Shakespeare
The Director's Cut

Michael Bogdanov is a theatre director of international repute. He has directed Shakespeare in many of the world's leading theatres and with major theatre companies including the Royal Shakespeare Company. He was Associate Director of the Royal National Theatre for eight years and he co-founded the English Shakespeare Company in 1986 with actor Michael Pennington. He was also Chief Executive of the Deutsches Schauspielhaus (National Theatre) in Hamburg, 1989–1992. He has won numerous awards at home and abroad including the Society of West End Theatres (SWET) Best Director for his production of *The Taming of the Shrew* (RSC) and the Lawrence Olivier Award for Best Director for his seven-play history cycle *The Wars of the Roses* (ESC). He lives in Cardiff, Wales.

Capercaillie Books

Shakespeare
The Director's Cut

**essays on Shakesperare's plays
volume 1**

Michael Bogdanov

Capercaillie Books

CAPERCAILLIE BOOKS LIMITED

Published by Capercaillie Books Limited,
Registered Office 48 North Castle Street, Edinburgh

© 2003 Capercaillie Books Limited

The moral right of the author has been asserted.

Design by Ian Kirkwood Design

Printed in Poland

Set in Cosmos and Veljovic

A catalogue record for this book is available from the British Library
ISBN 0-9545206-0-2

To Bill Wallis, Chris Dyer

and Michael Pennington

with whom I explored many of these ideas

Contents

Preface

Bogdanov's title should be his phrase 'The Bastards on the Rialto'. They may not be listed as characters in any production you may have seen but they are to be found on every page of this provocative and highly original series of essays. Forget about Shakespeare the romantic story-teller for, as in his many acclaimed, controversial and disturbing theatrical productions, what Bogdanov is doing here is helping us to identify the bastards in eight of the best loved plays. There is nothing gratuitous or fanciful about this excercise for Bogdanov's utterly convincing argument is inspired by his familiarity with the fullest versions of the texts. It was the bard himself who set his stories in a troubled and changing world in which dynastic imperialists and financial opportunists usually conspired to thwart individuals seeking what were thought of as idiosyncratic and inconvenient destinies. We are expertly and succinctly guided through the power nexus in all the plays discussed. We are left in no doubt as to the degree of Shakespeare's own anger, an anger Bogdanov has now memorably enabled us to share.

Professor Peter Stead, University of Glamorgan
writer and broadcaster

Introduction

I have a particularly strong affection for Leicester. It is the city where I first made a breakthrough in my thinking on Shakespeare. First with a lavish production of *Romeo and Juliet* at the newly opened Haymarket Theatre, and then at the Phoenix Theatre with what we called the '£94 Hamlet' – that sum being all we had to spend on the physical elements of the production. Scaffolding and wear your own clothes.

That production I did of *Romeo and Juliet* in 1974 had Jonathan Kent as Romeo, Alan Rickman as Paris, Mary Rutherford as Juliet and Bill Wallis as Mercutio. It was, for me, a seminal experience. In rehearsal the story had been coming over hard, clear and very exciting. Adrian Vaux had designed a very interesting modern steel structure for the set, and the costumes were uncompromisingly Renaissance.

When the production moved from the rehearsal room and arrived on to the stage, somehow the clarity and the hardness, the linear quality of the story, had gone. What was more, audiences weren't responding either to the production or the play. At the last moment, after the very final preview, I cut the whole of the end scene, where the Friar recaps the story for the benefit of Escalus and, after the death of Juliet, I switched to a press conference around the unveiling of the two gold statues that Capulet and Montague erect to the memory of each other's child.

Rock music built to a crescendo during a blackout and, when the lights came up, the entire company was assembled in modern dress in front of Romeo and Juliet, now dressed in gold cloaks and masks standing on the erstwhile tomb. Musak played. 'Fly Me to the Moon' . . . Escalus, the Duke, read the prologue as an epilogue from a cue card, as if inaugurating an unveiling ceremony. 'I hereby name this ship' . . . The main protagonists were photographed in front of the statues, shaking hands, the Nurse holding up a rope ladder, Escalus attempting to bring about the familial reconciliation with a three-way hand clasp. Jimmy Carter's smile of the time as he handed over the presidency to Reagan.

The transformation had an extraordinary effect. People in the audience shouted, people walked out, people cheered, people bravoed, people booed, and I thought 'For three hours they have been bored out of their minds and suddenly something has challenged them. A moment of real theatre.' It was an anarchic stroke and it turned the whole evening around in a most remarkable way. More importantly, it served to emphasise that I was going up the wrong path in attempting to ape what I thought was a traditional way of performing Shakespeare. There are many directors in many parts of the globe who are able to tell a Shakespeare story with tremendous power and clarity without having to go to the lengths that I have described, but that is how I discovered a way to tell the stories. By removing the barriers that exist between the language and the audience, by allowing them to identify with the characters clearly, by associating the events with contemporary politics, I allowed the plays to breathe. (I received more letters of complaint from apoplectic Colonels for my production of *The Taming of the Shrew* at the RSC than I ever did for *The Romans in Britain*).

The battle for modern dress has long been won. There were famous Barry Jackson and Tyrone Guthrie productions in the 1920s and 30s. In fact a critic recently applauded an Elizabethan dress production as a refreshing change. The argument has moved on to gender bending. All male – cos that's how Will did it; all female – cos that strikes a blow for equality; and role reversal – a white Patrick Stewart playing Othello in Washington with an all-black cast. I have no problem with any of this; theatre is the suspension of disbelief. But if, as in the case of all-male Shakespeare, it is in the name of experiencing the plays as they would have been performed in 1600, then I have a huge quarrel. It is impossible for us to receive the plays in any other form than a twenty-first-century appreciation of what is in front of us. All-male Shakespeare is just not our bag. So the only question that has to be answered is whether the plays themselves make sense textually, politically. . . . Claudius is still Claudius, Bolingbroke is still Bolingbroke, and Katherine is still the victim of a male wish-fulfilment dream of revenge, no matter what gender or mode of dress. No post-Burton/Taylor chauvinist romp will suffice, even when all parts are female.

Hamlet in 1975 was my first of five essays into the politics of the play. On the evidence of the gravediggers, Hamlet is thirty. Gertrude says he is 'fat and scant of breath'. The role was played for me in Leicester by the small, amply rotund figure of Bill Wallis. The play – and Hamlet's problem – opened up in a completely different way from that of the tall, thin, pale, haggard, meditative young prince of popular and traditional view. It posed a lot of awkward questions that the text had to answer. And it taught me an important lesson. That directing a Shakespeare play is like reading a detective story, piecing the clues together one by one, never taking anything for granted, ignoring received opinion – the narrative is of paramount importance. Also it taught me to look for those hidden moments, easily overlooked, that told the real story, moments that Stephan Greenblatt calls 'Invisible Bullets' (*Political Shakespeare,* ed. Jonathan Dolimore and Alan Sinfield, MUP, 1985). Was this the way to open up Shakespeare for a new generation of unengaged kids?

How do we deal with the plays in the twenty-first century in an increasingly multicultural society? And anyway has there ever been a time when these islands were not multicultural? I suspect that the courtyards of Elizabethan England teemed with 'masterless men', the tongues of a hundred regions grappling with the sound of a language comprised of the scraps and leftovers of a dozen other languages. Hard enough today for some people to distinguish Cork from Glasgow, Liverpool from Birmingham, Newcastle from Cardiff, Belfast from Bethnal. London then was the polyglottal stop-over for regional runaways, a bubbling linguistic British brew, the pot full of the still succulent sounds of French, Latin, Goedelic, Brythonic, Norwegian, Saxon, Platt-Deutsch, Hoch Deutsch, Middle-High Deutsch, fresh words entering the language (in a variety of spellings: Mr Shakesshaft, Shagsboar, Shakespear with or without an 'e') at a faster rate possibly than at any other time until the post-war American cultural invasion of Mr McDonald and the white-hot technological revolution. This hybrid, as yet unstandardised, form of communication where a society conversed in strange alien sibilants, dentals and palatals, eyes often bright with misunderstanding, formed the basis of a new language captured in the raw by Shakespeare and others and moulded into a mosaic of multifaceted storytelling. And this language carried a public health warning. It could kill. It was dangerous, a verbal contract sometimes taken out on one writer by another. Imprisonment was risked to attack public figures, the subjects of thinly veiled allegories set in Thebes, Athens, Verona, Venice.

My love of this and any language is a passion inherited from my father. In pre-revolutionary Russia before the turn of the twentieth century even, in the world in which my father grew up, the word was power. The balladeers, the pamphleteers, the poets, the novelists, the playwrights – those who could read and write held the key to the future. In a world of such devastating illiteracy, they were the truth. They were the word.

My father spoke English with consummate grammatical perfection, as only someone for whom it is not a native language can. And he had the vocabulary to match. Were he alive today he would be shocked to realise how many words that he used in everyday speech have already disappeared or are under threat. But this is the point, language must evolve. The battle for the survival of English in America is already on. An inexorable wave of Spanish is slowly flooding up the North American continent as the Mexicans take back by stealth what was taken from them by force. Los Angeles is already seventy-five per cent Spanish-speaking. What will the map look like in a hundred years' time? Already there is legislation against Spanish in some states, the first sign of a beleaguered minority about to dig in and fight a reactive battle against the force of time. What price Shakespeare in fifty to a hundred years? With hundreds of words dropping yearly out of use, what will be left of our understanding of his plays in centuries to come if we do not adopt a more radical attitude to these changes? Beowulf and Chaucer in translation – why not Shakespeare if it opens up the plays to the vast untapped energies of popular debate?

I was put off Shakespeare at school. We spent the whole of one term studying just one of Hamlet's soliloquies – 'How all occasions do inform against me.' We knew every comma, caesura, the etymology and derivation of every word backwards. Not a whiff of theatre in sight. Our English master was a Pickwickian character who read us chunks of Chaucer in what he informed us was the original accent – how did he know? It pained me to find that thirty years later my son was being taught in exactly the same way.

I didn't come back to Shakespeare until I was thirty myself. I had been eleven years in Ireland – Trinity College Dublin followed by a career in revue, musicals, variety, the folk scene and latterly a three-year stint as a TV Producer/Director with RTE (Radio Tefetis Eireann). I wished to return to theatre and realised that I would have to tackle the Shakespeare question. I went as an Assistant Director to where (I thought) they knew more about Shakespeare than anywhere else in the world – The Royal Shakespeare Company. I was the oldest assistant they had ever had. I soon realised that my political view of theatre and education, coupled with my experience at the sharper end of entertainment, was at odds with the dominant ideology there and left some eighteen months later to put my ideas into practice.

The intervening years have seen over fifty productions – some good, some bad, some ugly. Some plays I have directed four or five times in various parts of the globe – *Richard III, Hamlet, Romeo and Juliet, Macbeth* – each production an attempt to improve on the previous one and solve outstanding problems. (*The Tempest* I have directed five times but never get more than half right. The trouble is it's never the same half. I shall be doing it again.) Others – *Julius Caesar, Measure for Measure, The Taming of the Shrew, Timon of Athens* – I have done only once, achieving, I think, as much as I am able. As a director if you get it seventy-five per cent right you are world class. The English Shakespeare Company's *The Wars of the Roses* was some twenty-four hours of Shakespeare. Working on the seventy-five per cent basis, six hours were naff. That's two whole plays! (Opinions were divided as to which two.)

These essays do not attempt to analyse any of the productions. Indeed I do not even make reference to them. They are rather an attempt to set out the thinking that has informed my work over the years and in one case, *King Lear*, I have yet to attempt to scale the mountain. Enjoy. Or not, as the case may be.

Michael Bogdanov, September 2003

Hamlet

a northern European power struggle

Hamlet is the play that is buried most deeply in the English nation's consciousness. It is arguably the most famous play in the world, the most popular, the most quoted, the play that has given the English-speaking peoples a sizeable chunk of their vocabulary: 'to be or not to be', 'sweets for my sweet', ''tis brief as woman's love', 'something rotten in the state of Denmark', 'the rest is silence', and so on. It is seen variously as a play about the individual versus the state, freedom of choice, good and evil. It is a play of great soaring power and beauty in its language and at the same time a philosophical and theological debate about the meaning of existence.

It is also a play about a northern European power struggle. For no matter whether Hamlet is a homosexual misogynist, an Oedipal ditherer or a noble nutter, he is caught up in the mechanism of a great wheel that rolls inexorably over the Danish soil. Hamlet is the cog that comes loose in that great wheel and sends the Claudius steamroller careering downhill to crush them both at the feet of the conquering Norwegian army. And the straight fight between Hamlet and Claudius, the outsider versus the forces of the 'massy wheel', as Rosencrantz says, is the climax of a thrilling political story that often remains buried in a dungheap of psychological self-indulgence. In other words, familiarity with this language and the fact that *Hamlet* is one of the principal sources of cultural nourishment that drip feed the conservatism of educationalists and politicians alike, have helped to disguise the fact that it is one of the most powerful political plays of all time.

Hamlet, for the director, is a great whodunit. The art of detection lies in unravelling the mystery, following the clues, building up the evidence, deducing the story. On the surface, that story does not change: a series of events defines the parameters, whatever the year, whatever the century. To alter or omit some of these events is to redefine the story and therefore to alter the play that Shakespeare supposedly wrote. This is perfectly permissible, even desirable in the tradition of theatre as a living entity, something that grows organically, springing from the spirit of the time – indeed, the very way that Shakespeare arrived at his version of the story.

Ay, there's the rub, or 'the point', as Quarto One would have it. Will the real text of *Hamlet* please stand up? Quarto One consists of some 2,200 lines compared with Quarto Two's 3,800 – almost double – and is generally termed 'bad'. Bad and good: qualitative judgements implying a right and a wrong, for and against, inside and outside the law, acceptable and unacceptable.

Much post-war thinking has been influenced by the Lawrence Olivier film of *Hamlet*, which, coincidentally, also contained some two thousand lines. But with a crucial difference. The Olivier film managed to omit not only Fortinbras, but also Rosencrantz and Guildenstern, thus emphasising the disembodied quality of Hamlet's introspection. In other words, Olivier crucially changed the story of the play, as have recent productions by Matthew Warchus and Peter Brook, following in Olivier's footsteps and reducing the play to some two hours in length. They are therefore guilty of as much editorial corruption as those pirates accused, by generations of commentators, of corrupting Quarto One.

Fascinatingly, the objective storyline from Quarto One to Quarto Two through to the Folio presentation of 1623 has not altered. However, it is axiomatic that, whatever version is used, there are always many inconsistencies, not least of time, accidents of memory, improvisations by actors, insertions by commentators and 'tidying up' by editors. And, of course, there is that catch-all old argument that Shakespeare was not interested in detail, a convenient way of ignoring the collaborative process by which the performance was arrived at. But dramatically, for the practitioner, a loose end cannot be ignored as a matter of convenience because it does not fit in with a particular theory. It has to be tied up and bound tightly into the story.

Our tradition over the last century has been one of naturalistic detail. Audiences today demand a kind of logic. It is not a question of patting our heads and rubbing our theatrical tummies at the same time. An audience identifies with a piece of theatre at the point where it is performed. It does not say to itself 'that's what happened four hundred years ago'. If, for one moment, and one moment only, a point of contact and identification is made in the present, then the play immediately becomes a play of our time. That is why Shakespeare has been called the greatest living dramatist, and *Hamlet* the most enduring piece of *contemporary* theatre.

Bertolt Brecht's view of the play, written just after the Second World War in his *Short Organum for the Theatre* is as follows:

. . . the theatre should always be mindful of the needs of its time. Let us take, as an example, the old play of Hamlet. I believe that in the view of the bloody and gloomy times in which I am writing this, in view of the criminal ruling classes and general despair of reason, the story of this play may be read thus: it is a time of war. Hamlet's father, the King of Denmark, had, in a victorious war of plunder, killed the King of Norway. While the latter's son, Fortinbras, is preparing himself for a new war, the King of Denmark is also killed by his brother. The brothers of the dead kings, having become kings themselves, conclude peace with each other. Norwegian troops, on their way to a war of plunder against Poland, have been permitted to cross the Danish territory. Just at this time, the war-like Father's ghost asks young Hamlet to revenge the crime committed on himself. After some hesitation as to whether he should add one bloody deed to another, Hamlet – willing even to go into exile – meets at the seashore young Fortinbras and his troops on their way to Poland. Following his example, he turns back and, in a scene of barbaric slaughter, kills his uncle, his mother and himself, leaving Denmark to the Norwegians. Thus we observe how, in these circumstances, the young man, already somewhat stout, badly misuses his knowledge acquired at Wittenberg

University. This knowledge gets in the way when it comes to resolving the conflicts of the feudal world. His reason is impractical when faced with irrational reality. He falls a tragic victim to the discrepancy between his reasoning and his action.

'The theatre should always be mindful of the needs of its time.' Plays go in and out of focus, different aspects are suddenly high-lighted by contemporary events, shifts in global balance of power throw new light on old characters. Some years ago, *Hamlet* was the perfect Watergate play – bugs, tails, eavesdropping. (Q: What is the difference, in production terms, between a notebook and a pocket Dictaphone? An abacus and a calculator?) Polonius, grooming his son, Laertes, for potential office, has him tailed in Paris in order to 'by indirections find directions out'. Then, some eighteen years ago, the Captain's explanation of Fortinbras's march on Poland uncannily echoed the Falklands conflict, even down to the number of soldiers deployed and the description of the terrain. Hamlet comes over the hill and sees twenty thousand soldiers marching across the Danish plains. 'Good sir, whose powers are these?' (Incidentally if you were Prince Charles coming over the Sussex Downs and suddenly discov-ered twenty thousand foreign troops marching across your land, how would you react?)

CAPTAIN: We go to gain a little patch of ground
That hath in it no profit but the name.
To pay five ducats, five, I would not farm it;
Nor will it yield to Norway or the Pole
A ranker rate, should it be sold in fee.
HAMLET: Why, then the Polack will never defend it.
CAPTAIN: Yes, it is already garrisoned.
HAMLET: Two thousand souls and twenty thousand ducats
Will not debate the question of this straw.
This is th'imposthume of much wealth and peace,
That inward breaks, and shows no cause without
Why the man dies.

(Act IV, Scene iv)

Suddenly the resonances of this scene were immediate, the tensions were modern; the impact on the 1980s, electrifying.

> **HAMLET: Witness this army of such mass and charge,**
> **Exposing what is mortal and unsure**
> **To all that fortune, death, and danger dare,**
> **Even for an eggshell. Rightly to be great**
> **Is not to stir without great argument,**
> **But greatly to find quarrel in a straw**
> **When honour's at the stake . . .**
> **. . . I see**
> **The imminent death of twenty thousand men**
> **That for a fantasy and a trick of fame**
> **Go to their graves like beds, fight for a plot**
> **Whereon the numbers cannot try the cause,**
> **Which is not tomb enough and continent**
> **To hide the slain?**
>
> **(Act IV, Scene iv)**

Twenty thousand men, the exact number of the British Falklands task force, going to die for a patch of ground that isn't even big enough to bury the number of dead. What better description of that extraordinary last jingoistic fling of British imperialism?

Brecht, then, sees the story as a northern European power struggle. He omits, until the very end of his scenario, all the psychological and emotional complexity of the characters and relates only the events. Who on the basis of that analysis of the story would dare leave Fortinbras out of the play? The story would be destroyed, the political implication non-existent, the character of Claudius emasculated. Lawrence Olivier et al. have a lot to answer for. What story were they telling?

Is Brecht's version similarly biased, in as much as he leaves out other parts of the story to put a greater emphasis on his interpretation? And there's the rub. When facts are omitted to reshape the story to the particular interpretation, it becomes a new play.

Hamlet is still often read in terms of sick psychology. Either Hamlet has a paralysing fixation on his mother, or it is, to quote Olivier's film, 'the tragedy of a man who could not make up his mind'. The intellectual constitutionally incapable of acting. Or, to paraphrase Hegel, the noble art of revenge embraced by Greek tradgedy founders on the mundane rock of Christianity.

* * *

Let us look at the opening scenario, the wellspring from which the main action flows. Denmark is preparing for war, twenty-four hours a day, seven days a week, a round-the-clock arms race.

> **MARCELLUS:** . . . tell me that he knows,
> Why this same strict and most observant watch
> So nightly toils the subject of the land,
> And why such daily cast of brazen cannon
> And foreign mart for implements of war,
> Why such impress of shipwrights, whose sore task
> Does not divide the Sunday from the week.
> What might be toward that this sweaty haste
> Doth make the night joint-labourer with the day?

One can almost hear and see the roar of the blast furnaces, the Tornadoes, Exocets and Cruise Missiles rolling off the assembly lines, the troop ships being loaded, the cranes swinging the Shermans onto the quayside.

> **HORATIO:** . . . And this, I take it,
> Is the main motive of our preparations,
> The source of this our watch, and the chief head
> Of this posthaste and romage in the land.

> (Act I, Scene i)

Where is this heady atmosphere of war preparation, this 'posthaste and romage' ever reflected in performance? In Kozintov's Russian film version perhaps. Yet it is crucial for our understanding of

14

both the events that unfold and particularly of Claudius's motive for killing Old Hamlet. It is often cut, as in the production by Sir Richard Eyre, former Artistic Director of the Royal National Theatre, at the Royal Court Theatre, with Jonathan Pryce playing Hamlet, some years back. Royal acceptability. This huge essential piece of the jigsaw was missing from the very beginning. Try making sense of the picture after that.

As it happens, there is a case for reversing these speeches of Marcellus and Horatio. Horatio has only just returned from Wittenberg, ostensibly for the funeral of Hamlet's father, though Hamlet darkly hints it was for the marriage of Claudius and Gertrude. Hamlet has been in Elsinore some two months or thereabout. 'But two months dead, nay, not so much, not two!'

However, there is no reason for Horatio to hang around Elsinore for two months. If he *has* been there for two months, why has he not seen Hamlet before this? Of course, he may have gone back to Wittenberg and then returned again, but there is no evidence that he knows Hamlet well enough in Elsinore to drop in and see him as soon as he arrives. It takes a Ghost to do that. It would appear that however well Hamlet knew him in Wittenberg, Horatio probably lives in the equivalent of an Elsinore semi, presumably at college on the equivalent of a Danish Guild Scholarship from the local comp – classmate of Marcellus and Barnardo. The bright boy of the year. Wouldn't dream of dropping in at Buck House under normal circumstances. What doesn't seem to make sense is that an officer of the Guard, Marcellus, does not know why the military preparations are taking place and a student just returned from Wittenberg does. Further, Horatio says: 'The whisper goes so.' The soldiers would also have heard that 'whisper'. Hence the questions come better from the student just returned, mystified by the preparations, and it is the officer who is on the spot who gives the replies; and although later some editors give speeches to Horatio in Act IV, Scene i, there is no evidence that Claudius and Gertrude have any knowledge of Horatio. Not like those two nice boys from school, who came to tea once. What were their names? Rosamund and Gallimar? Send them a telegram, perhaps they can help.

So when do all these events take place that Horatio/Marcellus is describing? Thirty years ago. Source? The Gravediggers (this evidence is crucial on several counts). So what has Old Hamlet been doing for thirty years? It would appear, resting on his laurels, for now the forces are massing on the borders again, younger contenders (Norwegians, Polacks) eager for revenge, hungry to repossess lands they think is rightfully theirs.

> . . . Now, sir, young Fortinbras
> Of unimproved mettle hot and full,
> Hath in the skirts of Norway here and there
> Sharked up a list of lawless resolutes
> For food and diet to some enterprise
> That hath a stomach in't; which is no other,
> As it doth well appear unto our state,
> But to recover of us by strong hand
> And terms compulsatory those foresaid lands
> So by his father lost.

> (Act I, Scene i)

Are young Fortinbras's soldiers 'lawless resolutes'? Have they been 'sharked up in the skirts of Norway' ready for any 'enterprise that hath a stomach in it'? When we see them first, marching across Denmark to Poland, and then returning victorious – (Q: Why do they come back via Elsinore? They didn't go anywhere near it on the way to Poland) – it is clear that they are a highly professional, disciplined fighting machine. There is no evidence for this, merely deduction via the relationship of Fortinbras and the Captain, plus the discipline it takes to force-march across a continent, fight and win a battle on foreign ground, and return again (cf. the Falklands again). Are the comments of Horatio/Marcellus then merely biased patriotic propaganda? If so, they certainly are better in the mouth of Marcellus the soldier.

Thirty years of peace and now the threat of war. Is the following scenario possible?

CLAUDIUS: Put that bottle down brother, the situation is dangerous.

OLD HAMLET: Rubbish, I did it before, I'll do it again.
CLAUDIUS: But that was thirty years ago! Any day now
they'll attack and we'll be defending with bows and arrows!
We've got to . . .
OLD HAMLET: Just you leave it to me, old boy. Have a drink!

(A custom more honoured in the breach than the observance.)

Claudius could not leave it to his brother. There was not much point in Old Hamlet resting on what were now somewhat tatty military laurels. Denmark could be overrun at any minute. So Claudius killed him and took over. The theme of usurpation is one to which Shakespeare returns again and again in the plays, constantly proving that blood is not thicker than water. Brother kills brother, father betrays son, son kills father, cousin kills cousin. The Histories are a litany of fraternal and paternal slaughter.

To the end of his life the question fascinated him. (See the relationship of Prospero and Antonio in *The Tempest*.) Q: Did Claudius murder Hamlet for the love of Gertrude? Impossible. Nobody murders a king, kills a dictator, assassinates a president, and takes over the running of the country merely for love. Who wants all those problems of war, taxation, unemployment? Power must be wanted. Love of Gertrude there may have been, it is true, but there were other ways of sustaining love without giving himself the banging headache of running a country already in trouble. If you take over a country you take over all the problems that go with it. And Claudius is not negligent. He assumes the responsibility for the consequences of his action immediately, and sets the country on a war footing. He instantly dispatches two ambassadors, Voltimand and Cornelius, to Norway to tell them to cut it out:

> . . . to suppress
> His further gait herein, in that the levies,
> The lists, and full proportions are all made
> Out of his subject.

(Act I, Scene ii)

Power, and the nature of power, the use and abuse of it, usurpation, the territorial imperative, these are the themes.

* * *

Let us then examine the proposition that Hamlet should have been king. That he would have 'proved most royal, had he been put on'. This expectancy and rose of the fair state.

Thirty years. Hamlet is thirty.

> **HAMLET: How long hast thou been grave-maker?**
> **CLOWN: Of all the days i'th'year I came to't that day that our last King Hamlet overcame Fortinbras.**
> **HAMLET: How long is that since?**
> **CLOWN: Cannot you tell that? Every fool can tell that. It was that very day that young Hamlet was born – he that is mad, and sent into England . . . I have been sexton here, man and boy, thirty years.**
>
> **(Act V, Scene i)**

An auspicious double event, a cause for great national celebration – the defeat of the Norwegians and the birth of a future king, a red-letter day known by the whole population and presumably celebrated nation-wide. Not only that, the day the Gravedigger landed his job! No fallible memory this. And if that were not enough, the Gravedigger throws in another bit of proof – deduction this time.

> **HAMLET: How long will a man lie i'th'earth ere he rot?**
> **CLOWN: . . . Here's a skull now hath lien you i'th'earth three-and-twenty years.**
> **HAMLET: Whose was it?**
> **CLOWN: . . . This same skull, sir, was, sir, Yorick's skull, the King's jester.**
> **HAMLET: . . . I knew him, Horatio . . . He hath bore me on his back a thousand times . . . Here hung those lips that I**

**have kissed I know not how oft. Where be your gibes now?
Your gambols, your songs, your flashes of merriment that
were wont to set the table on a roar?**

(Act V, Scene i)

Twenty-three years in the earth. Carried Hamlet on his back a
thousand times. Hamlet remembers his jokes and his antics. He knew
him. It does not seem probable that he only knew him for, let us say,
one year, from the age of two and a half to three and a half, thus putting Hamlet's age at, say, twenty-six. His memory is longer, deeper
and fuller than that. The acquaintance is obviously a sustained one
and Hamlet's command of language sufficiently developed to appreciate his wit. Yorick died when Hamlet was seven. Hamlet is thirty. So
what is he doing at the age of thirty, still kicking around university at
Wittenberg? Why wasn't he around to take his share of responsibility
while all the problems were building up for his father at home?
Drinking too much, probably, talking rather than doing, and getting
fat.

The legacy of the thin, gaunt, pale young prince is a romantic one.
The part was written for Sir Richard Burbage at the age of thirty-seven
when, from the evidence of portraits, he weighed about seventeen
and a half stone. When Gertrude says 'he's fat and scant of breath',
she means just that. No pretending that 'fat' means 'sweaty' will do. In
all other contexts in Shakespeare, fat means fat. Sir John Falstaff
wasn't sweaty, he was fat. So was Sir Toby Belch. Yet the only reference to a fat Hamlet in performance is a caricature by Robert Dighton
in 1794 of Stephen Kemble in the part.

**HORATIO: You will lose this wager, my lord.
HAMLET: I do not think so. Since he went into France I have
been in continual practice.**

(Act V, Scene ii)

Continual practice? For the last three or four months all he has
done is run around the palace behaving like a lunatic. No sign of a
workout, jogging, the exercise bike. No wonder he's 'scant of breath'.

19

It begins to look as if Brecht was right.

So what is this 'expectancy and rose of the fair state'? Would he have 'proved most royal had be been put on'? (How does Fortinbras know? Did he ever meet him? Is he just saying nice things about the dead?) What evidence do we have that Hamlet is popular with the people, apart from Claudius's paranoia? After all, 'the rabble' shout 'choose we, Laertes shall be king'. Not 'bring back Hamlet'. Hamlet's lack of decision would certainly have landed Denmark in a right old mess.

> **QUEEN: I hoped thou shouldst have been my Hamlet's wife.**
> **I thought thy bride-bed to have decked, sweet maid,**
> **And not have strewed thy grave.**
>
> **(Act V, Scene i)**

Was this possible? How old was Ophelia? In Shakespeare's day, girls were marriageable at the age of twelve. Juliet was not yet fourteen (just like her mother) when marrying. Miranda was not much older, and she had been on a desert island all her life. At seventeen one was on the shelf. Even if we pitch Ophelia's age at sixteen there is still a fourteen-year age gap between Hamlet and Ophelia. So: what is the thirty-year-old heir to the throne doing messing around with the sixteen-year-old daughter of the Prime Minister? Laertes knows it is dangerous and that it will only end in tears. Polonius likewise. He cannot have a sexual scandal touch him. The liaison is impossible. Royalty must marry royalty. From all sides there is pressure.

> **LAERTES: . . . But you must fear,**
> **His greatness weighed, his will is not his own.**
> **For he himself is subject to his birth.**
> **He may not, as unvalued persons do,**
> **Carve for himself. For on his choice depends**
> **The safety and health of this whole state.**
> **And therefore must his choice be circumscribed**
> **Unto the voice and yielding of that body**
> **Whereof he is the head. Then, if he says he loves you,**
> **It fits your wisdom so far to believe it**

As he in his particular act and place
May give his saying deed; which is no further
Than the main voice of Denmark goes withal.

(Act I, Scene iii)

Hamlet may only marry the King's (and Queen's) choice. He may not 'carve' for himself! It would be a political disaster for Polonius to be involved in a court sex-scandal.

POLONIUS: I would not, in plain terms, from this time forth
Have you so slander any moment leisure
As to give words or talk with the Lord Hamlet.
Look to't, I charge you.

(Act I, Scene iii)

From the beginning we only see an unhappy girl with a brother and a father laying a very heavy scene upon her. There is no let-up, no escape. Repression and suppression are in the air. Ophelia is used and abused. Polonius dresses her up and sets a trap, using the poor, frightened, defenceless girl as bait, the implication being that Hamlet would try to seduce her and reveal all. Hands up all those who think Hamlet has slept with Ophelia, and why not? With no other person around (none that we can see at any rate) to advise her, to confide in, it is no wonder that Ophelia goes mad. Mentally, she is savagely raped. Hamlet's will not his own? Neither is Ophelia's. Polonius is completely uninterested in the disastrous effect his plot has had on the mind of his daughter. He brusquely brushes off her attempt to talk to him about the traumatic experience she has just undergone:

POLONIUS: . . . How now, Ophelia?
You need not tell us what Lord Hamlet said:
We heard it all.

(Act III, Scene i)

As to the brother – write to me, he says, 'Let me hear from you'; but there is no evidence that Laertes ever writes to Ophelia. A young

21

girl alone in a male world of high politics. Worse, the handsome young prince (now fat), whom she used to see round the castle when she was small, whom she hero-worshipped (he was a wonderful fencer in those days), who started flirting with her a while back when he noticed one day that the little girl with pigtails and braces on her teeth had suddenly grown up . . . this thirty-year-old prince, once the 'expectancy and rose of the fair state', is behaving in an extra-ordinary fashion. Her mind cannot cope. Sweets for the sweet? Gertrude hasn't spoken to her for months. Ducks into doorways when she sees her coming. Easy to say now it's too late.

'I hoped thou shouldst have been my Hamlet's wife'? No chance.

The precocious little upstart daughter of the Prime Minister got what was coming to her. Harsh? It's a tough world for a woman. After all, Gertrude has managed to stay at the centre of power, a wife of not one, but two kings. No one wants an ex-queen around the palace. Like Queen Margaret in *Richard III*, once a woman is no longer married to power, it is down the slippery pole. And so much for brother-ly love. Laertes did not even know what was happening to his sister.

Similarly, Polonius is right-hand man to not one king, but two. He manages to make the transition and be trusted.

> **POLONIUS: Hath there been such a time – I would fain know that –**
> **That I have positively said ''Tis so',**
> **When it proved otherwise?**
> **KING:** Not that I know.
> **POLONIUS: Take this from this, if this be otherwise.**
> **If circumstances lead me, I will find**
> **Where truth is hid, though it were hid indeed**
> **Within the centre.**
>
> (Act II, Scene ii)

There is an inescapable echo here of the Elizabethan CIA – oper-ated so efficiently by Burleigh and Walsingham, the one that did for Mary, Queen of Scots and many others.

No tedious old fool this. Rather a calculating, cunning, conniving politician who keeps tabs on everything and everyone, even putting a tail on his priggish son in Paris. His one mistake? To let personal family feelings interfere with an objective judgement, and then, unable to admit that he is wrong, careering headlong to his death in the relentless pursuit of the proof of his convictions. 'By indirections find directions out.' He found out all right. 'Thou knowest to be busy is some danger.'

* * *

Hamlet is one of the great existential plays. Throughout the canon Shakespeare is obsessed with the nature of action, how far short we fall of our own expectations of ourselves, the discrepancy between the thought of action and the act itself.

HAMLET: Oh God, I could be bounded in a nutshell and count myself a king of infinite space, were it not that I have bad dreams.

(Act II, Scene ii)

As long as we do not allow the imagination to take over, we are capable of anything. The man who succeeds is that man who says 'this is what I am going to do' and does it. The *Realpolitiker*. The pragmatist. Richard III, fine until his imagination takes over. Antonio, taking over Milan, after years of neglect by his brother, his only contribution in the final twenty minutes of the play to Prospero's attempt to elicit feelings of guilt from him, an objective appraisal of Caliban's financial worth. 'A queer fish and no doubt marketable.' Prospero, for whom everything happens in his head, taking revenge, re-ordering the Universe . . . until he wakes up from his dream.

So often Shakespeare poses a *status quo* against which he pits a protagonist. This protagonist usually smashes him or herself to pieces against the rock of state. The turtle is turned over on its back, before being righted and lumbering off on its reactionary way. What lessons have been learned? The pyramid of power remains intact, the territorial imperative is exercised once again in the name of justice, divine right, necessity of state, and so on. *Hamlet* begins with an act of usurpation by a man of action, and finishes with one.

When we first meet Claudius he is in control. He has killed the king and is himself king. He sets about running Denmark. Military preparations are made. Two ambassadors are dispatched with ultimata. Hamlet is told to stay at home in Elsinore. 'For your intent / In going back to school in Wittenberg / It is most retrograde to our desire' – after all, we can't have the rightful heir to the throne running around a foreign country, brooding on whether he should have been king, enlisting foreign support, returning with an army. 'Be as ourself in Denmark.' The 'massy wheel' is turning: as yet no spoke has been thrust in its mechanism, to bring it to a grinding halt. Gradually the antics of Hamlet begin to prey on Claudius's mind. By the time the ambassadors return he is more interested in news of Hamlet than in the news of Norway. And what a poser 'Old' Norway has set him! Voltimand and Cornelius arrive back waving a piece of paper that ostensibly says 'Peace in our time'. Not only has 'Old' Norway given Fortinbras more money, he has given him more soldiers in return for a promise not to go against Denmark, and, what's more, he has asked Claudius's permission to march across Denmark to fight Poland. What does Claudius do? Say no and risk Norway's anger? Say yes and have twenty thousand foreign troops on his soil? No wonder he is 'like a man to double business bound' and 'stands in pause' where he shall 'first begin and both neglects' (Act III, Scene iii).

Deal with Hamlet – or with Fortinbras? Claudius fiddles, Denmark burns, and Fortinbras ends up annexing Denmark as he annexed Poland, the usurper at the gates (so that's why he came back via Elsinore!).

> **FORTINBRAS: I have some rights of memory in this kingdom,**
> **Which now to claim my vantage doth invite me.**
>
> (Act V, Scene ii)

What rights? Oh yes, Hamlet did say something about that. 'I prophesy the election lights on Fortinbras.'

HORATIO: Of that I shall have also cause to speak,
And from his mouth whose voice will draw on more.

Too late, Horatio. It would not have made a jot of difference if Hamlet had 'prophesied' or not. Fortinbras is going to rule Denmark. He accomplishes it without bloodshed. That had been done for him. He will rule until the Danes decide they do not want a foreigner as their leader, then another act of deposition will follow, bloody or otherwise. The lesson of history is never learned. And just in case there is some public unrest, we'll make a show of Hamlet, place him high above stage.

HORATIO: But let this same be presently performed,
Even while men's minds are wild, lest more mischance
On plots and errors happen.

(Act V, Scene ii)

Pacify the people, the world loves a good state funeral.

* * *

To opt in or to opt out. What does Hamlet do? If he kills Claudius he will be king. Does he want to be? What sort of king would he be? A Caligula-type king? Would his humanitarian and egalitarian feelings have taken over? The levelling of beggars and kings? Certainly the arts might have flourished. Or would his ruthlessness have come to the fore? Viz., his callous treatment of Rosencrantz and Guildenstern, sending those two unfortunate nonentities gratuitously to their deaths, not near his conscience. Only at this stage, far too late, is his indecision over. He realises finally the value of taking responsibility for one's actions.

HAMLET: If it be now, 'tis not to come. If it be not to come, it will be now. If it be not now, yet it will come. The readiness is all.

(Act V, Scene ii)

Too late. In his death, far from avenging his father's murder, he only succeeds in bringing about what, thirty years earlier, his father had fought to avoid: Norway conquering Denmark. 'Thus conscience doth make cowards of us all.'

Action. Inaction. The final shoot-out between Hamlet and Claudius is inevitable. They begin poles apart but, as with the sound of marching feet coming closer to the gates of Elsinore, so Claudius and Hamlet come inexorably together.

> . . . O, 'tis most sweet
> **When in one line two crafts directly meet.**
>
> **(Act III, Scene iv)**

Indecision brings chaos, the winner is he who decides – and does it. The readiness is all. Existential.

* * *

> . . . such a sight as this
> **Becomes the field, but here shows much amiss.**
>
> **(Act V, Scene ii)**

Hamlet, mad for love? Mad in craft? Immaterial. His real/feigned madness destroys everything he comes in contact with, turns the world upside down. Polonius, mad to prove his theory. Ophelia, mad with grief, isolation, rejection. Laertes, mad for revenge. Claudius, conceiving a mad, convoluted plot with Laertes, involving poisoned bottles and foils. If ever a plan was bound to go wrong . . . By now the whole world is mad. Getrude drinking herself to an early grave; order restored by Fortinbras, a foreigner, taking over a country of which he has no need and on which he has no claim. 'I will rule with the olive and the sword,' says Alcibides in *Timon of Athens*. The trouble is – how much olive, how much sword? When will the purge start?

As with all detective stories there are many suspects and a number of culprits. As to who the real villain is – Claudius, Old Hamlet, Young Hamlet, Fortinbras, or the Ghost – it depends on how you interpret the story.

Oh yes, the Oedipus theme is pretty interesting too. And the one of what life is all about.

Romeo and Juliet

**a marriage of inconvenience
and social irresponsibility**

Any production of *Romeo and Juliet* must begin with an analysis of the social responsibility for the deaths of the two young people. The acceptance on the part of much critical thinking that the two lovers had to die in order to (a) reconcile their parents' hatred, and (b) show society the way forward, begs the question as to whether the deaths might have been avoided in the first place, and prompts a debate about such measures that could and should have been taken to stop the feuding in Verona's streets.

In other words – was the tragedy man-made? Did it stem from choices and decisions, taken at certain critical moments, by consenting adults, that were wrong or at best unthinking, governed by self-interest, muddled do-gooding, or whatever? Society is a past master at stable-door bolting, whether the shrill cries of outraged indignation are directed towards oil-spilling tankers, rail crashes, underground station fires, or famine. But whatever the size or nature of the disaster, the root cause is always human error, and, more often, human greed. And we know that when that first outcry of public indignation dies down, apathy and self-interest will reassert themselves and a new variant of the old catastrophe will reoccur. In the wake of public protest, legislation is sometimes rushed through in an outward display of governmental action, seemingly to prevent a repeat of a particular disaster. But where commercial interest is involved, these measures are usually half-hearted, half-baked and in effect an avoidance of political and social responsibility, with no long-term benefit.

Historically, orthodox criticism has enveloped the deaths of Romeo and Juliet in a romantic aura. Romeo swigs from a little bottle marked 'Poison' and the audience suspends its disbelief. What would be the reaction if Romeo stabbed a needle into his arm? This romantic interpretation stems from the very first words of the Prologue – a prolific source of misinterpretation. As with so many opening scenes, Shakespeare sets up a proposition that cries out to be challenged or a condition that is immediately contradicted by events:

> **Two households, both alike in dignity**
> **In fair Verona, where we lay our scene,**
> **From ancient grudge break to new mutiny,**
> **Where civil blood makes civil hands unclean.**
> **From forth the fatal loins of these two foes**
> **A pair of star-crossed lovers take their life;**
> **Whose misadventured piteous overthrows**
> **Do with their death bury their parents' strife.**
> **The fearful passage of their death-marked love,**
> **And the continuance of their parents' rage,**
> **Which, but their children's end, naught could remove,**
> **Is now the two hours' traffic of our stage;**
> **The which if you with patient ears attend,**
> **What here shall miss, our toil shall seek to mend.**
>
> **(Prologue)**

'Two households both alike in dignity': on examination, this proves not to be an accurate description of the two families, or rather the two heads of the families, Capulet and Montague. The language of Montague is cultured, elegant, conciliatory, well, how would you describe it? – dignified.

> **MONTAGUE: Many a morning hath he there been seen,**
> **With tears augmenting the fresh morning's dew,**
> **Adding to clouds more clouds with his deep sighs.**
> **But all so soon as the all-cheering sun**
> **Should in the farthest East begin to draw**
> **The shady curtains from Aurora's bed,**
> **Away from light steals home my heavy son,**
> **And private in his chamber pens himself,**

Shuts up his windows, locks fair daylight out,
And makes himself an artificial night.
Black and portentous must this humour prove
Unless good counsel may the cause remove.

(Act I, Scene i)

His speech shows an anxious concern for the welfare of his son and is couched in quietly lyrical language. And that's about it as far as Montague is concerned. We don't really hear any more of him. But Capulet?

CAPULET: God's bread! It makes me mad.
Day, night; hour, tide, time; work, play;
Alone, in company; still my care hath been
To have her matched. And having now provided
A gentleman of noble parentage,
Of fair demesnes, youthful, and nobly trained,
Stuffed, as they say, with honourable parts,
Proportioned as one's thought would wish a man –
And then to have a wretched puling fool,
A whining mammet, in her fortune's tender,
To answer 'I'll not wed, I cannot love;
I am too young, I pray you, pardon me'!
But, an you will not wed, I'll pardon you!
Graze where you will, you shall not house with me.
Look to't, think on't. I do not use to jest.
Thursday is near. Lay hand on heart. Advise.
An you be mine, I'll give you to my friend.
An you be not, hang, beg, starve, die in the streets,
For, by my soul, I'll ne'er acknowledge thee,
Nor what is mine shall never do thee good.
Trust to't. Bethink you. I'll not be forsworn.

(Act III, Scene v)

Not a lot of dignity there. Rather, the 'call a spade a spade' language of a middle-class businessman ruling his daughter with a rod of iron, blunt, hard, brutal, lacking any finesse. One-syllable words stabbing out, like his fingers, into the 'frail bark' of his daughter's mind and body. The contrast between Montague and Capulet could not be greater. Both alike in dignity? Not a bit, one dignified, yes, the other not. (All right – so dignity sometimes means social standing.)

'From ancient grudge break to new mutiny.' We never discover what this grudge is; the reasons for the feud are buried somewhere in the dark abysm of time. 'Three civil brawls make civil hands unclean', but why? How? What is it about? Merely the senseless repetitive Pavlovian hatred of one group for another without any foundation – not even religion, that traditional haven of hatred. Reasons forgotten. Merely a Montague so hit him. I was going into Lombard Street Studio in Dublin one day, a rehearsal space belonging to Trinity College. Two kids were passing by. One said to the other, peering in at the window, 'Only English bastards go in there.' I had to stop myself protesting, 'I'm not English,   honest. Russian and Welsh.' Pavlovian hatred.

'A pair of star-crossed lovers.' References to fate and destiny abound, principally from Romeo: '. . . he that hath the steerage of my course, direct my sail'; 'O, I am fortune's fool'; 'I defy you stars.' It is true that the deaths of Romeo and Juliet are caused by forces outside of their control. But these forces, these circumstances and events in which the pair find themselves caught up, are entirely man-made, and their deaths the result of a complete abdication on the part of society of all social responsibility. Their mistake, made because of youth and immaturity, was to place their trust in an adult world of competence. The choices and decisions that were taken on the part of those people they trusted (principally the Nurse and Friar Laurence), and who should have known better, are the real reasons why Romeo and Juliet died.

'Doth bury their parents' strife.' Oh yes? Has society altered? Have the rules changed? Montague and Capulet may be reconciled but what happens when another girl wishes to marry someone who is not the choice of her parents? Must she obey? Or elope, to be captured and punished? The tragedy of Romeo and Juliet will repeat itself again and again unless a society that allows women to be bartered to the highest bidder without choice can be reformed and humanised.

Where does Escalus, the prince, stand in all this? Who has the ultimate responsibility? Is it inevitable that only the deaths of Romeo and Juliet can 'bury their parents' strife'? What other measures could have been taken to stop the senseless feuding? Was Escalus too indulgent? Erecting gold statues won't change anything. Only laws of equality will.

'The two hours' traffic of our stage.' Shakespeare may have intended the play to be only two hours long when he started out to adapt the poem by Brook, the source of the plot, but in order to speak an unexpurgated text in that length of time, it would require a speed-run of the play as pacey as the bullet train from Tokyo to Kyoto.

On closer analysis then, there are questions raised by the Prologue which must be answered. Assumptions are made that are challenged directly by the events of the play, proving, if proof were needed, that to take what Shakespeare wrote at face value is often to miss the subtle social and psychological knife wound inflicted verbally on the body of conservative society.

* * *

Love is in the air – or at least, lust. When we first meet Romeo, he is pining, as it turns out, for Rosaline. But love?

> **ROMEO:** . . . **She'll not be hit**
> **With Cupid's arrow. She hath Dian's wit,**
> **And, in strong proof of chastity well armed,**
> **From love's weak childish bow she lives unharmed.**
> **She will not stay the siege of loving terms,**
> **Nor bide th'encounter of assailing eyes,**
> **Nor ope her lap to saint-seducing gold.**
> **O, she is rich in beauty; only poor**
> **That, when she dies, with beauty dies her store.**
>
> **(Act I, Scene i)**

Romeo has tried everything to get her into bed, but Rosaline is not going to come across. He even offers to pay for it: 'Nor ope her lap to saint-seducing gold.' Do girls in this society do the business for fifty crisp ones? 'Then she hath sworn that she will still live chaste?' asks Benvolio incredulously. Unbelievable.

> **ROMEO: She hath; and in that sparing makes huge waste.**

It is quite clear that Romeo is merely suffering from a severe case of sexual deprivation despite all his love-sick poetry. Benvolio knows the answer – gatecrash Capulet's party and grab a piece of the action. It is clear that the norm in this society is that the girls sleep with the boys and not to do so is a mite peculiar. Rosaline, a heterosexual anomaly, is holding out on Romeo and is going to make him suffer for it.

Romeo visits Friar Laurence to tell him of his new-found love for Juliet:

> **FRIAR:** . . . **then here I hit it right –**
> **Our Romeo hath not been in bed tonight.**
> **ROMEO: The last is true. The sweeter rest was mine.**
> **FRIAR: God pardon sin! Wast thou with Rosaline?**

The Friar immediately jumps to the conclusion that Romeo has cracked it at last. Who? Rosaline? Can't even remember what she looks like. But Juliet – this is for real.

> **FRIAR: But come, young waverer, come, go with me.**
> **In one respect I'll thy assistant be.**
> **For this alliance may so happy prove**
> **To turn your households' rancour to pure love.**
> **ROMEO: O, let us hence! I stand on sudden haste.**
> **FRIAR: Wisely and slow. They stumble that run fast.**

What did he say? Did I hear him aright? He's actually going to marry Romeo and Juliet without a second thought? It's only thirty seconds since he was chiding Romeo for 'doting, not for loving, pupil mine'. Chastising him for forgetting Rosaline so soon:

> **And art thou changed? Pronounce this sentence then:**
> **Women may fall when there's no strength in men.**
>> (Act II, Scene iii)

So that's it then for the Friar – women are sexual vampires. Noble, strong-willed men have to turn them back to the path of righteousness away from the fires of lust and lechery. 'Wisely and slow. They stumble that run fast' – Friar Laurence is running faster than them all, and 'stumbling' has got to be the order of the day. An ironic ending to the scene. In his position of authority, the Friar should have ascertained that there was, in fact, a serious basis for this new love of Romeo's life and offered to negotiate, on behalf of the young people, with the two families. True, it might 'turn their rancour to pure love', but not by marrying them in this hasty, ill-timed, clandestine fashion. Had he stopped to think, he might have known what an uproar it would cause. But the Church in this play is dressed only in a little brief authority. Births, marriages, deaths, confessions or 'shrift'; otherwise it's a herbalist. It is an act of gross irresponsibility on the part of the Friar to marry Romeo and Juliet clandestinely and in such haste, and the tragic events that unfold stem directly from this instantaneous, unthinking decision.

Sex is in the air. For the Nurse, Juliet represents surrogate licentiousness. She titillates and fantasises about Juliet lying on her back with legs in the air, and vicariously relives the pleasures of her youth through the fourteen-year-old body of Juliet (or the not quite fourteen-year-old body). On Lamass Eve, she is eligible. Get the baby factory rolling.

> **LADY CAPULET:**   **. . . By my count,**
> **I was your mother much upon these years**
> **That you are now a maid.**
>> (Act I, Scene iii)

So Lady Capulet was married even earlier. By the time she was fourteen, she was a mother, Juliet had already been born. Paris, asking for Juliet's hand, says 'Younger than she are happy mothers made.' Married at twelve, mother at thirteen. And Capulet replies, 'And marr'd too soon are those so early made.' Something strange there, he sounds a bit bitter, maybe his marriage to a twelve-year-old hasn't worked out so well. Lady Capulet is now twenty-eight at best. How old is Capulet? Fifty? Sixty?

> **CAPULET: [at the party] . . . you and I are past our dancing days.**
> **How long is't now since last yourself and I**
> **Were in a mask?**
> **COUSIN CAPULET: By'r Lady, thirty years.**
>
> **(Act I, Scene v)**

There is probably a gap of at least thirty years between Capulet and his wife, and is Juliet the only survivor in a long line of cot deaths?

> **Earth hath swallowed all my hopes but she;**
> **She's the hopeful lady of my earth.**
>
> **(Act I, Scene ii)**

There's a lot riding on Juliet. But certainly Capulet doesn't appear to be too happy that he married quite such a young girl himself.

However, sex is in the air. Woo her, gentle Paris, come to my party. Capulet joins in the titillation too:

> **At my poor house, look to behold this night**
> **Earth-treading stars that make the heaven light.**
> **Such comfort as do lusty young men feel**
> **When well-apparelled April on the heel**
> **Of limping winter treads, even such delight**
> **Among fresh female buds shall you this night**
> **Inherit at my house.**
>
> **(Act I, Scene ii)**

And Romeo goes to the party too. Why? Peer pressure? He doesn't have to. 'He that has the steerage of my course . . .' Nobody is steering him – apart from Mercutio and Benvolio. He chooses to go. Wilful. He sees Juliet, grabs a passing servant. Who's that? 'I know not, sir.' (Who is he – outside catering?)

'O, she doth teach the torches to burn bright!' From that decision stems the first real tension strand of the story. The first encounter of Romeo and Juliet linguistically leaps out of time and convention. The wooing sonnet is couched in religious imagery. The moment elevated to a higher plane than that of merely 'examining other beauties'. A deliberate contrast to the sexual quips and innuendo of the levelling language in the previous scenes.

> **JULIET: Good pilgrim, you do wrong your hand too much,**
> **Which mannerly devotion shows in this.**
> **For saints have hands that pilgrims' hands do touch,**
> **And palm to palm is holy palmers' kiss.**
> **ROMEO: Have not saints lips, and holy palmers too?**
> **JULIET: Ay, pilgrim, lips that they must use in prayer.**
> **ROMEO: O, then, dear saint, let lips do what hands do!**
> **They pray: grant thou, lest faith turn to despair.**
> **JULIET: Saints do not move, though grant for prayers' sake.**
> **ROMEO: Then move not while my prayer's effect I take.**
> **Thus from my lips, by thine my sin is purged.**
> **JULIET: Then have my lips the sin that they have took.**
> **ROMEO: Sin from my lips? O trespass sweetly urged!**
> **Give me my sin again.**
> **JULIET:**   **You kiss by th'book.**
>
>   **(Act I, Scene v)**

Whichever way you cut it, sonnet or not, blushing pilgrim's hand, holy palmers notwithstanding, within thirty seconds of meeting Juliet, Romeo is kissing her. Ten seconds later, he's kissing her again. All pretty normal really. And don't forget, 'He that can lay hold of her will have the chinks.' Worth a lot of money, that girl. But note the Nurse's terminology: 'Lay hold of her.' Later she will say of Paris: There is one who would lay knife aboard. A pirate, plundering and pillaging.

Sex is in the air. Post-party, Mercutio bawls raucous obscenities into the night, business as usual.

> **MERCUTIO: I conjure thee by Rosaline's bright eyes,**
> **By her high forehead and her scarlet lip,**
> **By her fine foot, straight leg, and quivering thigh,**
> **And the demesnes that there adjacent lie,**
> **That in thy likeness thou appear to us!**
> **BENVOLIO: An if he hear thee, thou wilt anger him.**
> **MERCUTIO:** . . . **'Twould anger him**
> **To raise a spirit in his mistress' circle**
> **Of some strange nature, letting it there stand**
>
> . . . . .
> **I conjure only but to raise up him.**
>
> . . . . .
> **O, Romeo, that she were, O, that she were,**
> **An open-arse and thou a poppering pear!**
>
> (Act II, Scene i)

Once again there is a deliberate juxtaposition of the obscene language and profanity of Mercutio and the beauty of the language in the balcony scene. How would an Elizabethan audience have responded to these obscenities? What 'business' would the actor playing Mercutio have indulged in? An intriguing problem for the modern director. Be true to instinct (and probably history) and hit it for all it's worth, or submit to the pressure of English hypocritical Puritanism, where the breasts of royalty are splurged all over the front pages and ministers are caught with their trousers down or knickers up, while Shakespeare, that 'upholder of saintly virtue', is censored. No prizes for guessing where I 'stand' (Shakespearean pun – see Nurse).

And what of Mercutio? Asexual, bisexual, homosexual, misogynist? Young, old, thin, fat? Does he leap around like a leprechaun (played like Puck?) or sit around like some fat alcoholic bar-fly weaving magic with words, mercurial of mind rather than body? Quicksilver. The one who talks rather than does. My money's on the overweight drinker at the bar, spinning Celtic yarns into the night.

Climb over twelve naked women to get to a bottle of stout. Beady after twelve pints or a couple of bottles of the red; pick a quarrel with a lightbulb.

* * *

The whole of the first part of the play is intent on building up an image of a young, macho society of swaggering swains, parties, street life, sexual promiscuity. A materialistic society based on the false values of fighting and fucking. This society collides head-on with the pure emotion that Romeo and Juliet feel for each other. Already the time is out of joint, they are out of step with the conventions and behaviour of their peer group. Love? Pooh! 'You speak like a green girl.' Think yourself lucky that 'a man of wax' is asking for your hand. Marriage, my girl, is about wealth and position.

Lawrence Stone says:

In the late Middle Ages, the 'nuclear family' of the 'landed elite' was no more than a loose core at the centre of a dense network of lineage and kin relationships. The reason for this is the preoccupation with the preservation, increase and transmission, through inheritance and marriage of the property and status of lineage, of the generations of ancestors stretching back into the remote past. The larger the property and status, and the more ancient the family encamped on its ancestral acres, the more intense was the preoccupation with the lineage, and thus the greater participation of the kin in the formation and daily life of the conjugal family. To understand the moral premises upon which such a society is based, it is necessary to rid ourselves of three modern, western, culture bound, preconceptions.

The first is that there is a clear dichotomy between marriage for interest, meaning money, status or power, and marriage for effect, meaning love, friendship or sexual attraction; and that the first is morally reprehensible. In the sixteenth century, no such distinction existed, and, if it did, effect was of secondary importance to interest, while

romantic love and lust were strongly condemned as ephemeral and irrational grounds for marriage. The second modern preconception is that sexual intercourse, unaccompanied by an emotional relationship, is immoral, and that marriage for interest is, therefore, a form of prostitution. The third is, that personal autonomy, the pursuit by the individual of his or her own happiness, is paramount, a claim justified by the theory that it in fact contributes to the well being of the group.

(*The Family, Sex and Marriage in England, 1500–1800*, London 1977)

To an Elizabethan audience, the tragedy of Romeo and Juliet, like that of Othello, lay not so much in their ill-starred romance, as in the way they brought destruction upon themselves by violating the norms of the society in which they lived. Property and power were the predominant issues, which governed negotiations for marriage, while the greatest fear, in a society so acutely conscious of status and hierarchy, was of alliance with a family of lower estate or degree than one's own.

Lady Capulet describes Paris:

This precious book of love, this unbound lover, To beautify him only lacks a cover.

(Act I, Scene iii)

Form therefore is all-important, content immaterial. Your marriage has nothing to do with you, it is a family matter. Now be a good girl and stop crying. 'For this drivelling love', says Mercutio, 'is like a great natural that runs lolling up and down to hide his bauble in a hole.' But Romeo has moved on. Hiding his bauble in any old hole is no longer his prime concern.

Why does Mercutio fight Tybalt? It's not his quarrel. Wilful. Irresponsible. It could only end in tears. Why does Romeo fight Tybalt? It is his quarrel, or is it? In that internecine male world of pride

40

and prejudice, the manly virtues have to be displayed, a friend avenged. But it is a choice. Mercutio chooses, and Romeo chooses. Juliet has a husband chosen for her, but also chooses to choose another. The men go along with the peacock laws of vanity. Juliet goes with her instinct, breaking the male law of non-choice. Brave, outspoken, practical, vulnerable, a female beacon of civil liberty in a dark, chauvinist world.

* * *

The contrast in the two lovers is apparent from their very first meeting. Romeo oblivious of the danger around him, his language, like his love, soaring on wings, daring death by twenty swords for one glimpse of his 'bright angel'. Romantic, impractical. Like a puppy. Juliet, concerned with the danger, practical, forthright, to the point. Declaring her love with a simple beauty before Romeo has the chance to. A modern, emancipated miss:

JULIET: Thou knowest the mask of night is on my face,
Else would a maiden blush bepaint my cheek
For that which thou hast heard me speak tonight.
Fain would I dwell on form – fain, fain deny
What I have spoke. But farewell compliment!
Dost thou love me? I know thou wilt say 'aye'.
And I will take thy word. Yet, if thou swearest,
Thou mayst prove false. At lovers' perjuries,
They say, Jove laughs. O gentle Romeo,
If thou dost love, pronounce it faithfully.
Or if thou thinkest I am too quickly won,
I'll frown, and be perverse, and say thee nay,
So thou wilt woo. But else, not for the world.
In truth, fair Montague, I am too fond,
And therefore thou mayst think my 'haviour light.
But trust me, gentleman, I'll prove more true

41

> Than those that have more cunning to be strange.
> I should have been more strange, I must confess,
> But that thou overheardest, ere I was ware,
> My true-love passion. Therefore pardon me,
> And not impute this yielding to light love,
> Which the dark night hath so discoverèd.
>
> (Act II, Scene ii)

A disarming directness and simplicity. Reversing the order of conventional behaviour. Nice girls don't proposition. They wait to be asked. Nonsense says Will. If you think and feel something, say it. Love isn't about playing games and social niceties. It's about honesty and equality. (Compare Miranda, *The Tempest*.) Juliet, organising the wedding, masterminding the plan, practical, a chip off the old parental block. Romeo bragging, Juliet silencing. Romeo sometimes like a spoilt child. Juliet sometimes like a gently chiding teacher. Humour is absolutely vital. Otherwise the story is a tedious tale of two over-earnest kids. Let them enjoy themselves for goodness' sake. This relationship, this balance, is maintained throughout the play and is reflected in their language. Romeo, impotent in the face of events, is swept along by the actions of others. Juliet, a determined figure of action, forces, wills things to work. Two youngsters attempting to make sense of a senseless world, a world in which they were ahead of their time.

* * *

Who can Romeo and Juliet turn to for help? In the play, it is the Nurse, a surrogate parent, Juliet's confidante, her companion, her adviser, to whom she turns. It seems that Lady Capulet has a tentative relationship with Juliet to say the least. She is probably jealous and too close in years to be much help. What should the Nurse have done? She certainly should not have encouraged the relationship. But this desire to extract vicarious pleasure from the thought (and act) of Juliet losing her virginity, leads her to abandon all sense of her position and her responsibility. After all, it's fun running around with rope ladders in order to climb moonlit walls and act as go-between, pass love notes and trinkets from one to the other. 'I am the drudge, and toil in your delight. / But you shall bear the burden soon at night' (nudge, nudge, wink, wink). She encourages the liaison with disastrous consequences. Juliet has had her fun. Romeo is banished and a husband who is not in the bed may as well be dead.

> **I think it best you marry with the County [Paris].**
> **O, he's a lovely gentleman!**
> **Romeo's a dishclout to him.**
>
> (Act III, Scene v)

'Is that what you really think?' 'Cross my heart and hope to die.' Total irresponsibility. Juliet is abandoned. The Nurse, having wrung the last drop out of her love, squeezed her emotions dry, tosses Juliet aside like a rag doll. The Nurse has had her fun. Back to the reality of a proper marriage, there's a good girl. Sleep tight.

Friar Laurence, confessor to both children, their spiritual advisor, Romeo's mentor, desperately attempts to cover up his mistake and compounds it even further. He conjures up a fantastical plot, fraught with so many difficulties that it was odds-on to fail. And what is it that he is asking a young girl to do? Take a potion that counterfeits death for forty-two hours and, when she wakes up, she'll be in a vault with the decomposing bodies of her uncles and aunts.

> **Take thou this vial . . .**
> **And this distilling liquor drink thou off;**
> **When presently through all thy veins shall run**
> **A cold and drowsy humour. . . .**
>
> **. . . . .**
>
> **No warmth, no breath, shall testify thou livest.**
> **The roses in thy lips and cheeks shall fade**
> **To wanny ashes, thy eyes' windows fall**
> **Like death when he shuts up the day of life.**

> Each part, deprived of supple government,
> Shall, stiff and stark and cold, appear like death.
> And in this borrowed likeness of shrunk death
> Thou shalt continue two-and-forty hours,
> And then awake as from a pleasant sleep.
>
> (Act IV, Scene i)

What sort of plan is that? It's crazy. And Juliet does as he suggests with a fortitude which is quite extraordinary.

The Friar, as the one having spiritual responsibility for the well-being of the children, should have known better. The Nurse, having material responsibility for Juliet, should have proceeded with equal caution. Love is not a game. All the events in the play could have been foreseen and averted. People make bad decisions and then use destiny, the fates, the heavens, the stars to excuse them. It is a play about social responsibility and existential choice. There is a social system operating where, unless specific fundamental reforms occur, just such a tragedy is waiting to happen again. This is a mercenary society, grasping, greedy, avaricious, uncaring, and any individual who pits him or herself against it, is doomed.

* * *

The overriding preoccupation of the Montagues and the Capulets is made clear in the aftermath of the tragedy when the two bereaved fathers promise to set up golden statues to each others' children.

> MONTAGUE: . . . I will raise her statue in pure gold,
> That whiles Verona by that name be known,
> There shall no figure at that rate be set
> As that of true and faithful Juliet.
> CAPULET: As rich shall Romeo's by his lady's lie.
>
> (Act V, Scene iii)

Even now, they choose to express their loss in monetary terms.

For the only way they can measure the value of their children is by financial sacrifice. But the children died because Capulet wanted more wealth and was prepared to disinherit Juliet if she refused to marry Paris, a relative of Prince Escalus, and thus move the family closer to the seat of power. Juliet is treated like a chattel by her father, a pawn in a game of power, whose feelings are of minimal interest to him. 'The most you wanted was her advancement', says the Friar, in a rare flash of insight.

In its commitment and extravagance, the passion of Romeo and Juliet stands out against a background of licentiousness, on the one hand, and commercial transaction (the usual preliminary to marriage), on the other. Capulet's speeches to his daughter are violent in their cruelty; he will be obeyed. Love is not part of the marriage bargain; he is pleased that he has found a suitable match:

> **A gentleman of noble parentage,**
> **Of fair demesnes, youthful, and nobly trained,**
> **Stuffed, as they say, with honourable parts.**
>
> > **(Act III, Scene v)**

And that is the extent of his interest in Juliet's welfare. Contrast the crocodile tears of melodramatic falsehood from the family, on the fake death of Juliet, with the real emotion of both Romeo and Juliet at their respective deaths.

Juliet is abandoned by her mother: 'Do what thou wilt for I have done with thee.' She is deserted by the Nurse: 'I think it best you marry with the County.' And the best the Friar can do is to come up with a cockeyed, crazy plan involving drugs and tombs. Admittedly he is at knife-point for the second time in twenty-four hours as both young people go to him in desperation for some way out of the mess that he has got them into. But there is no way out. His plan depends on too many unknowns, a desperate remedy for a desperate time. Capulet advances the marriage by one day. (It was already too quick, but he couldn't wait any longer to get his grasping, greedy hands on Paris's title.) The Friar's plan is blown. (Critics of the modern-dress school of thought point out that Friar John being locked up in a house of plague and therefore unable to deliver Friar Laurence's letter to Romeo is unbelievable. Friar Laurence would have faxed or phoned. Tant pis.)

And Romeo meanwhile? He is in Mantua still believing in fates and stars:

> If I may trust the flattering truth of sleep,
> My dreams presage some joyful news at hand.
> My bosom's lord sits lightly in his throne,
> And all this day, an unaccustomed spirit
> Lifts me above the ground with cheerful thoughts.
>
> (Act V, Scene i)

In the next moment, when he receives the news of Juliet's supposed death, there occurs one of those astonishing Shakespearean objective flashes of insight into the way the world wags, his real view of what surrounds him. In buying poison from an Apothecary to kill himself with, Romeo suddenly steps right outside the character of a wimpish, lovelorn loon, tossed hither and thither like flotsam and jetsam on the tide of man-made idiocy, and delivers a devastating comment on the society in which he finds himself. He pays the Apothecary:

> There is thy gold – worse poison to men's souls,
> Doing more murder in this loathsome world,
> Than these poor compounds that thou mayst not sell.
> I sell thee poison. Thou hast sold me none.
>
> (Act V, Scene i)

In this moment, he reveals a social conscience and an acute awareness of the motives of greed and avarice that dominate all thinking, a hitherto totally unseen side of the feud, an echo of his opening encounter with Benvolio. It is Shakespeare the egalitarian, the humanist at work. Romeo instinctively and ideologically comprehends the very root-rottenness at the base of not just Escalus's regime, but of all regimes that treat women like cattle at auction and put commerce before humanity. Compare Romeo's speech on gold with one from *Timon of Athens*:

> **TIMON: Gold? Yellow, glittering, precious gold?**
> **. . . . .**
> **. . . Thus much of this will make**
> **Black white, foul fair, wrong right,**
> **Base noble, old young, coward valient.**
> **. . .Why, this**
> **Will lug your priests and servants from your sides,**
> **Pluck stout men's pillows from below their heads.**
> **This yellow slave**
> **Will knit and break religions, bless th'accursed,**
> **Make the hoar leprosy adored, place thieves,**
> **And give them title, knee, and approbation,**
> **With senators on the bench. This is it**
> **That makes the wappened widow wed again –**
> **She, whom the spital-house and ulcerous sores**
> **Would cast the gorge at, this embalms and spices**
> **To th'April day again. Come, damned earth,**
> **Thou common whore of mankind, that puts odds**
> **Among the rout of nations, I will make thee**
> **Do thy right nature.**
>
> **(Act IV, Scene iii)**

Marx analysed it thus: money, as much as it possesses the ability to buy and appropriate everything, is the object most worth possessing. Money is the pimp between the desire and the desired, between life and man's means of living.

Shakespeare paints a brilliant picture of the nature of money. He brings out two properties in particular. One, money is the visible divinity, the transformation of all human and natural qualities into their opposites; their universal confusion and the inversion of things. Money brings together impossibilities. Two, money is the universal whore, the universal pimp of men and peoples. The inversion and confusion of all human and natural qualities. The divine power of money lies in its nature as the estranged and alienating specious essence of man which alienates itself by selling itself. It is the alienating capacity of mankind. But what I, as a man, cannot do – i.e. what all my individual powers cannot do, I can do with the help of money. Money therefore transforms each of these essential powers into something which it is not. Into its opposite.

Money is both a pimp and a whore, the real poison in the world.

I am not trying to make out a case for Romeo being an early Marxist (or am I?). But as with so many of the visible and invisible bullets in the plays, here, in this little scene with the Apothecary, in Romeo's statement of gold being the real poisoner, the real murderer in the world, we have the real story of why Romeo and Juliet died. And recognising this reality, the scales drop from Romeo's eyes: 'I defy you stars.' He has reached the existential point arrived at by so many of Shakespeare's protagonists, where the realisation sets in that one's destiny is in one's own hands and in no one else's.

No stars, no heavens, no Fates. 'Tomorrow, and tomorrow, and tomorrow.' 'The readiness is all.' 'We are such stuff as dreams are made on.' 'On, on, if not to heaven, then hand in hand to hell.' Romeo is now a man of action. He will buy poison, go to Verona, prise open the tomb, die with Juliet – decision at last. No longer 'fortune's fool'. And nobody will get the blame. The Friar is exonerated. Escalus says to him, 'We still have known thee for a holy man.' At least in the Brook poem from which Shakespeare took the original story, Friar Laurence is banished for his part in the tragedy. But no, there are no scapegoats in Verona; everything, as is customary in politics, is smoothed over. Important to present a united front in these matters.

And those gold statues will atone. They cost a lot of money.

The Tempest

in the cold light of day – exile and dreams of revenge

In *The Tempest* old Shakespearian friends meet for the last time: man of action friend, man of imagination friend, nature versus nurture friend, usurpation friend, theatrical friend, power friend. A man sits in exile in a café in Paris, Prague, Miami, Bogota – and dreams of revenge on those who have booted him out of his kingdom. It is a waking dream, a sleeping dream, a daymare, a nightmare. He wakes up, pays for his coffee, his croissant. Goes off down the street, maybe picks up a cigarette butt, or if you are Imelda, tries on one of a thousand shoes. Nothing has changed, he is still the same, others are still in charge. He is still in exile, the café table his world, his distracted mind his globe.

> **O God, I could be bounded in a nutshell and count myself a king of infinite space, were it not that I have bad dreams.**
> **(*Hamlet*, Act II, Scene ii)**

I was once standing in a toilet in Neary's bar in Dublin and there was a man standing next to me doing what is necessary. A great, big, broad hunk of a fella in a shabby suit, and he said to me 'I'm the King of Connaught.' 'I beg your pardon?', I said. 'I'm the fuckin' King of Connaught.' (Don't ask me why the King of Connaught spoke with a Dublin accent but he did.) 'And do you know where the King of Munster is?' 'No', I said. 'He lives in a bungalow in Brighton.' So I thought, Well, yes, all right, so the King of Munster lives in a bungalow in Brighton, I suppose that's the fate of contemporary Irish kings

49

who have no hope of ever inheriting the land again. But somewhere in Brighton the King of Munster is still sitting there with his sword and insignia, hoping and pretending that there is life after republicanism.

So exile could be anywhere. It could be a café table, it could be lying in bed, on top of a bus, it could be a desert island. It could be Brighton.

The magic of the island as represented by Ariel and Caliban and the restoring of harmony to a disordered universe by the old wizard himself, have conditioned critical thinking on *The Tempest* for almost four centuries. This thinking, along with the classification of the play as a romance, has successfully served to disguise the fact that *The Tempest* is a vicious play about a wish-fulfilment dream of political revenge. The story is simple.

Prospero, the ex-Duke of Milan, is obsessed with his brother, Antonio, who has usurped his position as Duke, and with those who have aided him, principally an old enemy, Alonso the King of Naples along with his brother Sebastian. It is yet another turn of the old screw that Shakespeare uses in earlier plays: the theme of the usurping brother, of blood not being thicker than water, and so on. But this time it is a political killing rather than a literal one. Usually a brother kills a brother to take over the throne, whether it is Claudius killing Old Hamlet or Richard III killing everybody. Here, Antonio metaphorically 'kills' Prospero by sending him into exile. Everything that happens in the play stems from that one act of usurpation. Prospero then sits in a bungalow in Brighton for twelve years, brooding on revenge. That is the story. Simple.

Napoleon on Elba:

What was left to him? No future, only ultimate death on the island. How could this extraordinary man adapt himself to this position? After activity and glory on such a heroic scale how could he be content to do nothing but wait patiently for death? How impotent, frustrated, and hopeless he must have felt. A magnificent past, an impotent present, a hopeless future. How could he pass the time? He made a definite effort and buried himself in his memories, but how futile

these reminiscences of past greatness and glory as contrasted with his present circumstances. An ordinary man may have submitted and adapted himself to the situation, but not an extraordinary man such as the Emperor.

(James Kemble, *Napoeon Immortal*, 1959)

The ambivalent heart of *The Tempest*'s fantastical mosaic leads to some of the most bizarre productions of any of Shakespeare's plays and to the widest possible divergences of opinion as to its meaning. And, because it is a play about imagination, it invites that imagination to run riot in such a way that the staging of no two *Tempests* is ever alike. That is both the strength of the play and its weakness. This weakness manifests itself in production as a lack of a coherent political centre, and accordingly many productions resort to peripherals to try and demonstrate what a particular director thinks was going on in Shakespeare's mind at the particular time in his life when the play was written.

Now it is clear that Caliban and Ariel are two quite extraordinary creations that have come to fascinate people through the ages – performers, directors, critics, academics – to the point where the play has been seen to be only about Caliban and Ariel and a bunch of boring lords. They are always called 'boring lords' – and (inadvertently) are often played as such. But the problem with 'those boring lords' (of whom let us not forget Prospero is one) is that they occupy three-quarters of the play. Now, if they are that boring, what is it in the play that is so exciting? You may as well get rid of them (some productions do), and be left with some weird play – about the psyche and psychoanalysis, the id and the ego, the bestiality of man versus the spiritual – that lasts about an hour.

The Tempest is supposedly Shakespeare's last play with just a chunk of *Henry VIII* to follow. It is, I suppose, inevitable that his artistic farewell would be interpreted down through the ages as Shakespeare's 'swan song', 'the death of the artist' (one of the most consistent interpretations), and the final lines of the Epilogue as a plea for forgiveness for all that the artist creates. Prospero's staff is seen as the muse: once it is broken, and the muse has deserted the artist, he/she stands alone, a bare forked animal – 'What strength I have's mine own.' Ultimately the fate of the artist to succeed or fail lies in the hands of those people who respond to his or her work. A broken staff is no defence against critical opprobrium. So, it has been seen as Shakespeare retiring to enjoy the autumnal twilight of his life in the golden glow of his orchard in Stratford-upon-Avon, looking back over his life and forgiving those critics who have been less than favourably disposed towards his works. A play of nostalgia and regret, and personal battles with the ego, the spirit, the body, and so on. All these allegorical interpretations hold water up to a point, but only to half-way up the bottle; there is too much air at the top. Yet the clues as to the structure are laid out in a very clear trail right the way through the entire canon of plays from the very moment that Shakespeare first explodes into the round world of the Elizabethan 'O'.

* * *

The very first clue is in the title itself – *The Tempest*. Just about everybody recognises now, although this is a recent acknowledgement, that the tempest is not simply an elemental storm during which a real boat is shipwrecked. More important, the play is concerned with the tempest of the mind, or of the soul, a deep psychological trauma that is induced through the releasing of the subconscious either by natural means – sleep and dreams – or through some kind of self-induced hallucinatory experience. A brainstorm. Lear, mad on the heath, identifies with the elemental storm, 'the tempest in my mind'. There is a moment in *Richard III* when Richard's imprisoned brother, George, Duke of Clarence, just prior to his murder by Richard's hired hit-men, wakes up and describes his nightmare to his jailer, Brackenbury: 'O then began the tempest to my soul.' That 'tempest to the soul', his nightmare of death by drowning at the hands of his brother, is the starting point of the play, *The Tempest*. But it is now Prospero's soul that is tempestuously in turmoil.

Now sleep and dreams are, in essence, the key words of *The Tempest*. 'Sleep' occurs some thirty-odd times, and 'dream' forty times, and speeches based on waking or sleeping are dotted throughout the play, permeating the atmosphere:

> **We are such stuff**
> **As dreams are made on; and our little life**
> **Is rounded with a sleep.**
>
> **(Act IV, Scene i)**

We are concerned here with the power of an imagination that is released by dreaming, the power of the mind to conceive of things that, paradoxically, the mind does not even comprehend. It is this boundless infinity of the imagination, a consequence of all our thoughts, our hopes, and aspirations, that Shakespeare analyses. But the power of man to accomplish what he achieves in those dreams is not infinite, it is very finite. Put more simply, it's the discrepancy once again between the thought of action and the act itself.

This tempest of the soul, this dream of Prospero's is the same dream that we all have, for example, when, on being sacked from our job, we go out of the office and think of what we should have said. How we should have cut the boss, the teacher, the tax inspector, down to size, stood up for our rights. In any situation in which we are humiliated by someone more powerful, we experience a well of frustration, of impotence, of injustice, of anger that surges up through our souls and we replay that moment of humiliation over and over again, inventing for ourselves a completely different scenario of what we should have done, of what we should have said, of how we would handle the situation if it were ever to happen again. It does not obscure the fact, however, that we are still standing outside that office door having got the sack, fantasising about how we should have taken over the firm, the country, the universe ourselves. In other words it is that same wish-fulfilment dream of Prospero's to reinstate himself as Duke of Milan that is at the very heart of *The Tempest*.

In our dreams we can all win the Olympic hundred metres in a world record time – do it in our heads. I've just done it. I've just done it again! The actuality of it is that this morning I ran up and down on the spot 140 times and took five minutes to do it (in an effort to get fit – again!). The actuality, of course, is 'bounded in a nutshell'; it is the narrowest channel of thought that corresponds to how we perform.

> **When the down-trodden underling has to yield to circumstance and to take things lying down, he dreams of himself standing up for his rights and being victorious. He did not realise that he had it in him until he dreamed of himself actually living that role. The very fact of having that dream boosts his self-esteem: he squares his shoulders, is encouraged to have another shot at it, and he comes out successfully. Thus a dream is not merely a wish, it is an encouragement and inspiration. Because it shows a man what he can be, it enables him to become so. The dream is not merely wishful thinking, it is creative and purposive; it does not merely allow us to sleep in the night, it encourages us to action in the day.**
>
> **(J.A. Hadfield, *Dreams and Nightmares*, 1954, p. 29)**

I talk constantly in these essays of the man of action, the *Realpolitiker*, the man who seizes the moment, the man who is capable of extending his capacity along the lines that correspond to what he is capable of conceiving in his mind. Antonio is that man in this play. Antonio is the man of action, Prospero of inaction caught half-way between his responsibilities as a leader of the state and other intellectual pursuits that lead him to be a bad ruler.

This is one of the prime tenets of the piece – that the regime of Prospero was obviously on the slippery slope. The similarity is with the rule of Old Hamlet, or Richard II – the state or country is on the slide, and therefore the need to reinstate firm government, to re-establish the *status quo*, is seen by those surrounding the leaders – a brother and a king, in this instance – as an opportunity to move in and right the tottering regime.

The island that Prospero inhabits in his mind is an island of insularity, but it is also the world, it is also the cosmos. That island, as Jan

Kott says in *Shakespeare Our Contemporary* is winter, it is summer, it is spring, it is autumn. It is barren, it is fertile. It is rocks and lunar land-scape, it is bowers and flowers. It expands and contracts in our minds according to outlook and attitude. In other words, we are looking at the universality of a problem, but through the personal eyes of a man who at this moment is suffering from the deprivation of his position of authority. Prospero is a Tzar of Russia, the Shah of Persia, a political prisoner, frustrated, angry and bitter, unable to return. The real, true meaning of exile. Banished ('Banishment?' says Romeo – 'Do not say "banishment"!' – 'Be merciful, say "death"'), forever cut off from the culture, the society, the people, the roots that you understand, unable to return to the place of your birth or your culture. That is the situa-tion that Prospero finds himself in.

This then is a dream of wish-fulfilment revenge that might occur in anybody. Merely to apply to the play the theory of the artist in the twi-light of his career asking for forgiveness for his work misses the social and political centre of the piece, and relegates the play to the realm of soporific romanticism.

* * *

The story begins with the lives of a bunch of usurpers being placed in the hands of an artisan, a boatswain. 'What care these roarers for the name of king?' This is fundamental. Political order is reversed – all the wealth, power and position of the royal party are as nothing. They are forced to rely on 'hard-handed men' whose trade is the rope and the sail. 'My kingdom for a horse.' Shakespeare the great leveller. Then, at the point when the boat goes down and the lords are about to be killed, what miracle happens? Bang! Not even wet, not even spoiled in any way. Lifted out, dumped on dry land, clothes coloured brighter than bright, as if the whole bunch had been on a 'midnight mushrump' binge. Miraculously, just like that. Just as they're about to drown I go 'bang' and I've saved them. There they are. In my head.

My desire for revenge wants to see them dead, drowned. But the problem with that is I would be left on my own, still without power, without position. So I'll torture them further. Humiliate them – I want them to fall in front of me on their knees and humble themselves, beg my forgiveness and give me back my dukedom. I'm not going to let them drown with the boat, I'm going to drive them through hell and back to make their lives a misery until I'm ready. Prospero accordingly proceeds to make a vicious use of his imagination and terrorise his foes in the guise of Ariel, the agent of his mind, a figure akin to a barbaric instrument of torture, the process of thought operating at the speed of light.

The storm, the brainstorm – the 'tempest to the soul' – calms somewhat and the story begins. We learn who Prospero is, who these boring lords are, and lo and behold they are about as boring as a bunch of rattlesnakes. Prospero, in his head becomes a man of action, the impotence of exile banished. He says what he's going to do and then proceeds to do it. A series of mirror images permeates the play: master and slave, power and weakness. The acquisitive nature of Antonio grabbing the crown is mirrored in the clowns, Trinculo and Stephano, grabbing the trinkets. Right the way from the bottom of the ladder up, everybody is on the make, fighting to be top dog, and whatever rung they reach, they are concerned only with booting those beneath them further down. So with Trinculo and Stephano.

Even before Prospero's deposition by Antonio there is an act of usurpation. Prospero the arid, Prospero the intellectual, Prospero, back in Milan, the academic, subdues Prospero the bestial, the animal, the natural, the instinctive. Post-Antonio yet another act of usurpation; that of the island. Prospero, deposing Caliban, creating him his slave. Caliban, part Prospero's animalism, part symbol of those foreign territories that had been captured and explored by Elizabethan sailors plundering the Indies, discovering strange islands inhabited by wild, primitive peoples and enslaving them; strange animals that are brought back and exhibited in the streets, as Trinculo says, 'for a piece of gold'.

Prospero in his head conjures up a boat in a storm. On board are all his enemies. More important, it contains his brother Antonio who, in collusion with the King of Naples, has booted him into exile. Not killed this time, just one minuscule humanitarian stage further back. After all he's no danger. And what a story he tells Miranda, his daughter! (Does she exist back in Milan? Or is she too part of his wish-fulfilment?) This 'good old man' renowned for the liberal arts, this aesthete, the leading intellectual of his time (so he says), left the running of the state to his brother.

Consider the following scenario.

> **ANTONIO: Prospero, there are three million unemployed, a hundred thousand businesses going bust. The pound has been devalued twenty-five per cent. A quarter of a million people are homeless and all you do is worry about what Wittgenstein really meant!**
> **PROSPERO: Don't bother me now, Tony, I am just perfecting a disappearing dove. Have you got a silk handkerchief? (You old sorcerer you!)**

No wonder his brother took over. Prospero? His library was 'dukedom large enough'. And now Antonio has ruled for twelve years. No one has got rid of him, he was too clever, did a deal with the King of Naples to leave him alone.

> **PROSPERO: Of temporal royalties**
> **He thinks me now incapable, . . .**

(me – with reason)

> **   . . . confederates –**
> **So dry he was for sway – wi'th'King of Naples**
> **To give him annual tribute, do him homage,**
> **Subject his coronet to his crown, and bend**
> **The dukedom, yet unbowed – alas, poor Milan –**
> **To most ignoble stooping.**
> **   . . . . .**

MIRANDA: Wherefore did they not
That hour destroy us?
PROSPERO: Well demanded, wench.
My tale provokes that question. Dear, they durst not;
So dear the love my people bore me;

(proof, please!)

A mark so bloody on the business, but
With colours fairer painted their foul ends.
In few, they hurried us aboard a bark,
Bore us some leagues to sea, where they prepared
A rotten carcass of a butt, not rigged,
Nor tackle, sail, nor mast. The very rats
Instinctively have quit it.
　　　　　. . . . .
MIRANDA: 　　　　　How came we ashore?
PROSPERO: By Providence divine.
Some food we had, and fresh water, that
A noble Neapolitan, Gonzalo,
Out of his charity, who being then appointed
Master of this design, did give us, . . .

(So they are not going to starve, and presumably it must have been
at least a month's supplies. No point else.)

　　　　　　　　　　　. . . with
Rich garments, linens, stuffs, and necessaries
Which since have steaded much. . . .

(I see, quite a Harvey Nicks full!)

　　　　　　　　　. . . So, of his gentleness,
Knowing I loved my books, he furnished me,
From mine own library with volumes that
I prize above my dukedom.

　　　　　　　　　　　(Act I, Scene ii)

Prospero's tale emerges as biased and emotional. And why not? After all, it has taken him twelve years to tell it. This rotten carcass of a boat, this leaky hulk, this rat-quitting bark, suddenly expands, becomes larger and larger, like the fisherman's tale in the adage. The fissures are suddenly caulked up, the bilges are baled, and it finally ends up as something of a three-masted schooner. Food, water, rich garments, linens, stuffs, necessaries, books from his library 'which since have steaded much'. Sounds like he should have applied for an export licence. And do we think that Gonzalo would have risked his life to do all this unauthorised? Prospero thinks so. More probably it was by design, otherwise Antonio might just as well have killed them. And Miranda? What is her memory of all this?

> 'Tis far off,
> And rather like a dream than an assurance
> . . . Had I not
> Four or five women once that tended me?
>
> (Act I, Scene ii)

This worries Prospero. If Miranda recalls this experience, perhaps she remembers the real events of twelve years ago. No. Thank goodness. He can tell the story his way. But the important thing about Miranda's memory is that her one recollection is of privilege. Nurture has already tainted her. She has inherited a sense of class difference, there can be no fresh start. Despite her innocence her language to Caliban is appalling:

> MIRANDA: Abhorred slave,
> Which any print of goodness wilt not take,
> Being capable of all ill! I pitied thee,
> Took pains to make thee speak . . .
>   . . . when thou didst not, savage,
> Know thine own meaning, but wouldst gabble like
> A thing most brutish, I endowed thy purposes
> With words that made them known. But thy vile race,
>   . . . had that in't which good natures
> Could not abide to be with. Therefore wast thou

> **Deservedly confined into this rock, who hadst**
> **Deserved more than a prison.**
>
> > (Act I, Scene ii)

No wonder some editors give the speech to Prospero – too distasteful, otherwise.

Why a daughter? Why not a son? Impossible. His revenge is surrogate. In his dream his daughter will marry the son of the king. This son will himself be king one day. She, herself now queen, will bear a son who will be king. Prospero's revenge will be complete. His grandson will rule Milan and Naples. This is Prospero's goal, the grooming of Miranda. This will be his revenge. But for Miranda, the memory of the first two and a half years is fatal. Her place in a male world of privilege and power is already ordained.

The chess game:

> **MIRANDA: Sweet lord, you play me false.**
> **FERDINAND:** **No, my dearest love,**
> **I would not for the world.**
> **MIRANDA: Yes, for a score of kingdoms you should wrangle,**
> **And I would call it fair play.**
>
> > (Act V, Scene i)

Whatever you do – cheat, lie, brag, corrupt, kill, conquer – I will support you. Prospero has lost her. That game of chess, a metaphor for the power politics of the world, sums it all up. Foot-soldiers are overwhelmed, the castle stormed, the knights and bishops overthrown, the king captured. The queen will call it fair play, whichever way it is accomplished. Ends and means. Miranda has already accepted the corrupting force of the territorial imperative. Everything is legitimate if it is accomplished in the name of power and possession. The Antonios of this world. In that one small nugget of a scene, Miranda legitimises her uncle's behaviour as Prospero admits to himself the inevitability of might over right. It is a frightening moment when Miranda steps out from the cell, looks at the courtiers, Antonio and Sebastian, the thugs, the sharks, the villains, who have done her father down, and says:

> **O brave new world,**
> **That has such people in't!**

(Act V, Scene i)

''Tis new to thee', says Prospero. He knows she is soon to be corrupted. Since he is not able to be part of it himself, it is an irony that Prospero will send Miranda back to Milan to swim in that shark-infested pool. It is a cynical view of the world: if you can't beat them, join them. Miranda, as Ferdinand's queen, will take her place in a formal, corrupt society that only knows how to play by certain rules. If you don't play by those rules, you don't win. Prospero didn't win, but his daughter will. But at least if she can't be king she can be the next best thing, queen, and, maybe, a mother of kings. In Shakespeare's society the only way for women to have power was to be next to the source of power. If you are Gertrude, in *Hamlet*, and you manage to marry two kings, you stay where you have the influence. It is a society where women are bartered to the highest bidder. A harsh world, a hard world. One that sickened Shakespeare. No wonder his plays deal with dreams and change.

* * *

So where does Caliban, that 'debauched' fish, fit into the dream?

> **Evidence of archaic images is found in our bodies, carrying about with them traces of their archaic ancestry. Our aquatic ancestry, for instance, survives not only in the persistence of gills as the Eustachian tube connecting the mouth with the ear, but also in the fact that in our veins there flows a stream of blood plasma which consists of practically the same constituents, sodium, potassium, and calcium, and nearly all the same proportion, as sea water, which it originally was. As with our bodies, so with our minds – we carry**

61

about with us archaic modes of thinking and of behaviour. Have we not all at times been astounded at the bizarre thoughts that occur to our minds, at the shocking desires which sometimes possess us, and at the irrational impulses that sway us against our volition? They come 'out of the blue' of our radical unconscious and are quite alien to our ordinary civilised modes of thinking. It is not surprising that St Augustine thanks God that he was not responsible for his dreams!

(J.A Hadfield, *Dreams and Nightmares*, 1954)

Caliban is that suppressed side of Prospero's sexual nature, the cock that has to be chained, the incestuous feelings of a single man for his daughter, alone together on a desert island for twelve years. Miranda is now fifteen, sleeps alone. Has to, Prospero dare not trust himself.

Hadfield says,

This collective unconscious, says Jung, consists of the 'inherited potentialities of human imagination'. 'It is the all-controlling deposit of ancestral experiences from untold millions of years, the echo of prehistoric world events to which each century adds an infinitesimal small amount of variation and differentiation. These primordial images are the most ancient, universal, and deep thoughts of mankind.' The collective unconscious therefore 'contains not only every beautiful and great thought and feeling of humanity, but also every deed of shame and devilry of which human beings have ever been capable.' The collective unconscious constantly affects our habits and behaviour quite unknown to ourselves, for 'it is a determining constituent of all experiences'.

(Ibid.)

Caliban the cock, Caliban the cannibal, the primitive, has to be subdued, colonised. Caliban the man, no fish – 'legged like a man', 'fins like arms', 'the third man that e'er I sighed for'. Ferdinand, too, has to be chained up like Caliban, his sexual desires (and Miranda's) too strong to be let loose. Show them a masque (this would please the court, particularly King James).

The play, after all, moves towards a wedding, and the most palpable example we see of the magician's powers is the anaesthetised betrothal masque, presided over by Juno, where the lusty Venus and her destructive son Cupid have been banished from the scene. But the performance is also preceded by the most dire warnings against sexuality:

> **PROSPERO: If thou dost break her virgin-knot before**
> **All sanctimonious ceremonies may**
> **With full and holy rite be ministered**
> **No sweet aspersion shall the heavens let fall**
> **To make this contract grow; but barren hate,**
> **Sour-eyed disdain and discord shall bestrew**
> **The union of your bed with weeds so loathly**
> **That you shall hate it both. Therefore take heed.**

Male sexuality this time: all the lust is presumed to be Ferdinand's, whilst Miranda remains Prospero's innocent child. Ferdinand's reassuring reply, an overly emphatic protestation of chastity, includes submerged fantasies of rape and more than a hint that when the lust of the wedding night cools, so will his marital devotion:

> **. . . the murkiest den,**
> **The most opportune place, the strong'st suggestion**
> **Our worser genius can, shall never melt**
> **Mine honour into lust, to take away**
> **The edge of that day's celebration . . .**
>
> **(Act IV, Scene i)**

This is the other side of the assumption that all women at heart are whores: all men at heart are rapists – Caliban, Ferdinand, and of course that means Prospero too.

* * *

The Tempest has been subject to these doubts, subversions and reversals not only because part of its subject is colonisation. The play would have been put on the defensive anyway if only because the master–slave relationship of Prospero/Caliban is openly subject to racist interpretation. No amount of noble savage will do.

And Ariel, that malicious needle of darting light – the vicious revenge-exacting agent of Prospero's thought-process (no gentle spiriting here) – is enslaved to Prospero in the same way:

> **. . . I will rend an oak**
> **And peg thee in his knotty entrails, till**
> **Thou hast howled away twelve winters.**

> **(Act I, Scene ii)**

Prospero's mind is trapped in the thought of vengeance, and until that vengeance has been exacted, he cannot relax. His mind is twisted in bitter torment. Only when he has smashed and pummelled his enemies into submission can Ariel be released from that torment, from that 'cleft pine' that he has inhabited for twelve years. Twelve years. The exact time that Prospero has been in exile, his head trapped in the pine and pain of the past. Only when he has purged himself of those feelings can he release his mind from the bonds that bind it. Be free. Move forward. It has taken him twelve years to tell Miranda the story.

The play progresses in a very clear pattern of vengeance for power taken and power to be regained. And there is haste, there is speed. Time is not on Prospero's side. Time is not on your side when, in your dream, you run to catch the train, and, with the train gradually pulling away, you sprint like mad to keep up with it. Sometimes you succeed in jumping on and you breathe a sigh of relief. Sometimes you relax and say 'Too bad, I've missed it', and wake up. The time element of the dream is absolutely crucial – there is haste, there is

64

speed – Prospero's plans have to be accomplished within a certain time-span – what's the time, what's the time? Two o'clock, three o'clock, four o'clock. It must be done by six o'clock.

> **ARIEL: Is there more toil? . . .**
> **Let me remember thee what thou hast promised,**
> **Which is not yet performed me.**
> **PROSPERO:** How now, moody?
> **What is't thou canst demand?**
> **ARIEL:** My liberty.
> **PROSPERO: Before the time be out? No more.**

Prospero himself wants rid of this pain, this turmoil, but there will be no let-up in the torment until he has purged himself of the hate and frustration, waking in a cold sweat of reality. Before the time be out? Impossible. Trapped in a nightmare of his own making.

'Freedom, highday, highday, freedom.' 'Get a new master, get a new man.' Take these chains from my mind and set me free. By six o'clock. Sebastian and Antonio would murder Alonso – brothers in arms. Trinculo and Stephano would murder Prospero. Wake up! Wake up!

Correspondingly, through this mirror imagery, the time-span of the play may be that of an afternoon performance on a stage, artificially, in front of an audience. That artificiality, that act of creation of a piece of theatre that we see mirrored in the time of the real world, is, yet again, the acceptance that a play is like a dream, that it is not real – that spectators and actors alike are drawn into a relationship with each other suspending disbelief together in a unifying act that is broken and smashed the moment the performance is ended and the audience exits into the street. On that stage, we've fought for crowns and battled with monsters, we've created fantastical images and wrestled for kingdoms, but we go out into the dark of a city night, among the tin cans and the rubbish and the lorries belching out fumes. Out into reality. In other words, nothing has changed; only, for a short period of time, we have suspended ourselves in animation before going back out into the real world.

So it is with Prospero, so it is with the performance – the two things running parallel. Prospero does not have much time, he has the length of the dream in which to accomplish everything. But when Prospero, having gone through this exorcism, finally goes back into the real world, he will be the same old Prospero who was booted out of Milan. The same old man sitting on the park bench. The same old Russian waiter in exile. The same old heir to the Romanian throne fighting with somebody in a garret in New York over who is next in line to take over. He's me, still doing my 140 running-on-the-spot jogging exercises. He's the King of Munster in his bungalow in Brighton.

* * *

And so to the final scene. Why didn't Prospero finish off Antonio, Sebastian and Alonso while he had the chance? He was too soft. That is why he will never return to Milan and regain his dukedom. If he did, Antonio would take it all over again. He, Antonio, had no need to kill Prospero. He knew that Prospero was too ineffectual to be able to combat him.

> **MIRANDA:**   **Wherefore did they not**
> **That hour destroy us?**
> **PROSPERO:**   **. . . Dear, they durst not.**
> > **(Act I, Scene ii)**

Durst not? That man? What a joke. Prospero has a need to kill Antonio, but he doesn't – he forgives him. Wrong. As the dream starts to fade, as morning approaches, as his mind starts to clear, so the effort of the night is banished and the desire for total revenge fades.

> **PROSPERO:**   **. . . The charm dissolves apace.**
> **And as the morning steals upon the night,**
> **Melting the darkness, so their rising senses**

> Begin to chase the ignorant fumes that mantle
> Their clearer reason.

(Act v, Scene i)

And throughout the final scene, during these waking moments, as the mind swims up into consciousness to take in the ugly industrial wasteland of a world that is there instead of the desert island, so Prospero's strength ebbs too. From being at first bewildered and disbelieving, he finds the arrogance of the court reasserting itself. As 'miracle' succeeds 'miracle', so the revelations become commonplace. It is like attempting to keep up with modern technology. Wonders will cease. Prospero doubts himself. They doubt him. Dressed in his everyday clothes he is no longer a magician. His staff is broken, his strength is his own, which is most faint. And, as this insubstantial pageant fades leaving not a wrack behind, so he is left at his café table, on his bench, in his bed.

And Antonio? No begging forgiveness for him. 'Ha ha, brother', says Prospero, 'Bet you're sorry now.' Not a bit of it. Antonio says nothing in the last scene except to comment on the commercial viability of exploiting Caliban.

> SEBASTIAN: Ha, ha!
> What things are these, my lord Antonio?
> Will money buy 'em?
> ANTONIO: Very like. One of them
> Is a plain fish, and no doubt marketable.

(Act V, Scene i)

The nature of Antonio has not changed one iota. He is still the synthesis of *Realpolitik*, of Machiavelli, as Prospero has known very well all along. In that one (a plain fish and no doubt marketable) line, as so often is the case in the final scenes of Shakespeare's plays, a bullet is fired with a ferocity that shatters all illusion. No play about forgiveness this. The fundamental clash is between the man of action and the man of imagination. The polarity of the canon itself. As long as we believe in a system of acquisition and exploitation, the Antonios will always

triumph over the Prosperos. Let W.H. Auden have the last word from
The Sea and the Mirror:

As all the pigs have turned back into men
And the sky is auspicious and the sea
Calm as a clock, we can all go home again.

Yes, it undoubtedly looks as if we
Could take life as easily now as tales
Write ever-after: not only are the

Two heads silhouetted against the sails
– And kissing, of course – well built, but the lean
Fool is quite a person, the fingernails

Of the dear old butler for once quite clean,
And the royal passengers quite as good
As rustics, perhaps better, for they mean

What they say, without, as a rustic would,
Casting reflections on the courtly crew.
Yes, Brother Prospero, your grouping could

Not be more effective: given a few
Incomplete objects and a nice warm day,
What a lot a little music can do.

Dotted about the deck they doze or play,
Your loyal subjects all, grateful enough
To know their place and believe what you say.

Antonio, sweet brother, has to laugh.
How easy you have made it to refuse
Peace to your greatness! Break your wand in half,

The fragments will join; burn your books or lose
Them in the sea, they will soon reappear
Not even damaged: as long as I choose

To wear my fashion, whatever you wear
Is a magic robe; while I stand outside
Your circle, the will to charm is still there.

As I exist so shall you be denied,
Forced to remain our melancholy mentor,
The grown-up man, the adult in his pride,

Never have time to curl up at the centre
Time turns on when completely reconciled,
Never become and therefore never enter
The green occluded pasture as a child.

> *Your all is partial, Prospero;*
> *My will is all my own:*
> *Your need to love shall never know*
> *Me: I am I, Antonio,*
> *By choice myself alone.*

So that, then, is *The Tempest*. Scenic splendour, allegory, what you will, the various pieces of the jigsaw must fit together. Written in the sparest of language, each gem an intricate and delicate facet of a jeweller's mosaic, it is a revenge dream of enormous political potency. It is once more the perennial struggle for power, the gulf that exists between thought and action that we see in *Hamlet*, that we see in *Richard III*, that we see in *Timon*, that we see in Shakespeare's plays played out on a stage all over the world. Man fighting man for greed and gain, for who is to have the ultimate say in government. Fighting for the crock of gold that lies at the top of the pyramid of power. Jan Kott's grand mechanism, the escalator shuttling the contenders up to the top until they reach out and topple off the edge. And at the same time there is another system to be comprehended, another way of ruling; that life cannot always be this perennial struggle to put the boot in the faces of those who are weakest. That somewhere there is a system – maybe it is that of Gonzalo – the commonwealth system, based on Montaigne and his theories of fertility and abundance and shared organic growth. No machines, no science, although this is a commune with a king (Gonzalo's mind does not stretch as far as a

Marxist redistribution of power and wealth). Here, the final imaginative leap has not been made. But maybe it is a world where those who toil, where those who use their hands and not their minds are the real kings of the universe – 'The master, the swabber, the boatswain, and I, / The gunner and his mate.' What use is ambition and morality if 'Imperious Caesar, dead and turned to clay, / Might stop a hole to keep the wind away' (*Hamlet*, Act V, Scene i)?

Ambition. We could all end up as a piece of clay stuck in a hole in a wall to stop the wind coming through. Buried in *The Tempest*, once again, is that strange, not even subconscious feeling from Shakespeare that something else must be there to put in the place of this extraordinary avaricious existence and brutalising system of government. 'My ending is despair.'

The Merchant of Venice

if money be the food of love...

What makes *The Merchant of Venice* at one and the same time so fascinating and so repugnant? Anti-Semitic it isn't – anti-racist it is. It has been lumped in with other plays as a romantic comedy, presumably because it results in three pairings and three marriages, a girl impersonates a judge and there is multiple mayhem over some ring swapping. Oh yes, and there's that hilarious scene of a Jew trying to cut a pound of flesh off nearest to a man's heart. Has them rolling in the aisles, that one. Of course, once that nasty man Shylock is out of the way we can get on with resolving the love stories. But who carves who up?

The romantic view. A young girl wanting to marry someone forbidden by her faith elopes disguised as a young man, taking with her money for survival. A young Venetian, desperate to win the hand of the wealthy lady he loves, borrows money to visit her and, in an inspired piece of guesswork, hazards all on the least likely of three caskets to contain her portrait. His best friend falls in love at first sight with milady's maid.

The cynical view. A Christian layabout of little faith persuades a young Jewish girl to leave her father, steal from him a fair size of his fortune in the process, and change her religion. A profligate gambler borrows money to buy himself a ticket to spot-the-lady in one of three caskets and gets lucky. An urban yob hitches himself to the maid of the aforementioned rich lady on five minutes' acquaintance on condition that the aforementioned gamble pays off. If not – ciao.

71

To subscribe to the romantic view one has to ignore the warning sign: Danger – Shakespeare At Work. The play may be set in Venice and based on an old Italian story but it presents a devastating picture of the emergent merchant capitalism of the Elizabethan era. Chivalry is dead (did it ever exist other than as a concept?) and London laddism rules. Racism, class, money – Shakespeare nails them all to the consumer pinboard.

Venice – a world centre of commerce. The Rialto – a medieval stock exchange where merchants come to trade. They're a right bunch of bastards on the Rialto. It's all that fast money, easy come easy go, desperate dealing, FTSE, NASDAQ, Dow-Jones, names that jump straight out of a Potter spell. It's not that Shylock doesn't behave badly, but if you drive a dog into a corner don't be surprised if it bites you.

It has been argued that given Shakespeare's Catholicism and the Elizabethan attitude to usury, audiences in 1600 would have seen nothing wrong in the treatment of Shylock as a Jew. This historical view of the play ignores the accuracy with which Shakespeare prefigured and fingered Thatcher's Children and the twenty-first century's obsession with consumerism and market forces. Broken oaths, broken promises, wild speculation, betting, wagering, betraying, deceiving – *The Merchant of Venice*, masquerading as a romantic comedy, leaves an unsavoury trail of capitalism and racism in its wake. Not much hope then for the various marriages floating precariously on this Venetian Lagoon of mercenary opportunism.

* * *

Let us look at the givens.

Bassanio, a layabout lad-about-town, is broke. Not only broke, he has squandered the money he borrowed from Antonio, a rich merchant venturer, and now is on the cadge again:

> I owe you much, and like a wilful youth,
> That which I owe is lost; but if you please
> To shoot another arrow that self way
> Which you did shoot the first, I do not doubt,
> As I will watch the aim, or to find both
> Or bring your latter hazard back again
> And thankfully rest debtor for the first.
>
> (Act I, Scene i)

But this time he is determined to sort himself out once and for all. If Antonio will stake him again he will try and win the hand and fortunes of a rich heiress, Portia. This is not the first time he has tried this ruse.

> BASSANIO: In my schooldays, when I had lost one shaft,
> I shot his fellow of the self-same flight
> The self-same way, with more advised watch,
> To find the other forth; and by adventuring both
> I oft found both.
>
> (Act I, Scene i)

It's all about show, a con. Arrive in town with a retinue of servants, a new suit, a flashy tie, and pretend to be something you are not. The Italian and French Rivieras used to be full of such seeming gentlemen, gently easing rich spinsters and widows out of their fortunes by playing the class card.

The clue to the real social status of Bassanio comes with his sidekick, Gratiano, a bit of rough straight out of the champagne-swilling, jumped-up, get-rich-quick city yob culture. Gratiano hitches a ride on Bassanio's Belmont charm chariot, making off in the process with Portia's maid – contingent of course on Bassanio securing the prized Portia.

> BASSANIO: . . . But hear thee, Gratiano:
> Thou art too wild, too rude and bold of voice,
> Parts that become thee happily enough
> And in such eyes as ours appear not faults,

But where thou art not known, why there they show
Something too liberal. Pray thee take pain
To allay with some cold drops of modesty
Thy skipping spirit, lest through thy wild behaviour
I be misconstered in the place I go to,
And lose my hopes.

(Act II, Scene ii)

And how much does Bassanio need from Antonio for this further throw of the dice? This second arrow?

PORTIA: What sum owes he the Jew?
BASSANIO: For me, three thousand ducats.
PORTIA: What, no more?
Pay him six thousand, and deface the bond.
Double six thousand and then treble that . . .

(Act III, Scene ii)

Three thousand ducats. Three thousand ducats!? Is that all, says Portia when she finds out, is that all I am worth? You've put a man's life in jeopardy for a paltry three thousand ducats? Thrice three times and it would still be an insult.

Portia is seriously rich, Bassanio is seriously out of it. From now on the trousers will be firmly on the female. Bassanio will probably only be allowed pocket money.

Antonio, however, wealthy though he may be, does not have the money – it is a question of cash flow. Speculate to accumulate. International trade. His wealth is all ventures abroad. When his ships come home he will be worth a fortune, but for the moment it is all collateral. Antonio's WASP-like world is a self-protective club, a lodge of Masons, the MCC, the Garrick, Balliol and Trinity – one falls, we all fall.

ANTONIO: I am a tainted wether of the flock,
Meetest for death. The weakest kind of fruit
Drops earliest to the ground, and so let me.

(Act IV, Scene i)

74

Bond and bind together, help each other out. No punitive interest rates here but plenty of golden handshakes. Corporate business. Globalisation. Antonio believes he must be sacrificed for the health of the club.

In such a world outsiders are not just unwelcome, they are positively discriminated against. Never mind Jews – Germans, French, Moroccan, Spanish, Eastern, Scots (lot of North of the Border prejudice running around in Elizabeth's reign) and – to make sure nobody gets off – the English, all are despised and verbally if not literally spat on. Colour, race, creed – who cares? If your face doesn't fit, forget it. 'Let all of his complexion choose me so.' Lucky that Bassanio (is he one of ours?), braggart, penniless gold-digger that he is, is out of the right drawer.

* * *

Much has been made of the homosexual current coursing between Antonio and Bassanio, although it appears to be decidedly one-way. Antonio playing Cyrano to Bassanio's Christian. Winning the lady's love in pounds in place of poetry. But this time Cyrano is in love with Christian, not Roxane. As Christian climbs the balcony to claim the kiss won by Cyrano's voice, so Bassanio besieges Belmont with Antonio's money.

Antonio the loser. Antonio the symbol of closed class wealth. Antonio, the older man in love with the younger. It must hurt. Is this the real reason for Antonio's sadness in the opening scene? He knows that Bassanio is on the woo again.

**Well, tell me now what lady is the same
To whom you swore a secret pilgrimage . . .**

(Act I, Scene i)

Solanio and Salerio (salt – rub it in), those gossiping muppets on the Rialto, touch on it nearly. Solanio: 'Why then you are in love.' Antonio: 'Fie, fie' (The Merchant doth protest too much methinks!) A lot of jealously around, bitchiness, emotional blackmail.

BASSANIO: [reads] . . . all debts are cleared between you and
I if I might but see you at my death. Not withstanding, use
your pleasure. If your love do not persuade you to come, let
not my letter.

(Act III, Scene iii)

How do you measure love? With a pound of flesh? Or a ring?
Antonio cannot believe, having narrowly escaped losing his life, that
Bassanio is unwilling to part with the ring given him by Portia as pay-
ment to Balthasar/Judge. Just as Portia asks the question of Bassanio
over the sum of three thousand ducats (what's my love worth?), so
Antonio asks it over the ring.

ANTONIO: My Lord Bassanio, let him have the ring.
Let his deservings, and my love withal,
Be valued 'gainst your wife's commandèment.

(Act IV, Scene I)

Are you measuring my love for you against Portia's in the form of
a ring? And Bassanio gives it away. An oath broken. Light love,
easily given away as a pair of socks. Shylock refused to break his oath.
He had made it in the eyes of the Lord and such is his faith that he
expects the Christians to understand.

SHYLOCK: An oath, an oath! I have an oath in heaven;
Shall I lay perjury upon my soul?
No, not for Venice!

(Act IV, Scene i)

But the Christians swear, take oaths, make vows of marriage that
are worthless. This Christian world is not one of faith, but of Bank
Holidays where Whitsun is celebrated not according to the religious
calendar but on the last Monday in May. Yet Antonio is a nice man, a
gentle man, a noble man, it just so happens that he hates and despises Jews – 'our sacred nation' – spits on them, spurns them, calls
them misbelievers, cut-throat dogs, voids his rheum upon their beard.

76

Nothing wrong with that is there? Doesn't stop him being 'a nice man', 'a gentle man', 'a noble man', does it?

As for Shylock, that's a different matter. His daughter Jessica calls her home a hell. Yet the only time we see Shylock and Jessica together he treats her with trust and civility, giving over to her keeping the keys and custody of his house. He doesn't lock her in and forbid her to go out, merely asks her to make his house safe from Christians on a carnival rampage. In fact, compared with some other fathers of our Shakespearean acquaintance, Shylock's regime seems pretty lax. Jessica obviously has had plenty of opportunity to meet, play and sport with Lorenzo. Of course she may have climbed out of the window and spent nights on the tiles while Shylock thought she was safely tucked up in her little bed or swotting for GCSEs. The 'hell' of her home seems more like the hell of a teenager's home without TV and stereo – and no tobacco, alcohol or exstasy if you please. (To some, this would smack of responsible parenting.)

Her envy of the life of the young Christians on the Rialto is palpable – she can't wait to join them. No stifling orthodox Judaism for her. Get out there and live a little as soon as she can. And while she's about it she'll take a load of money and jewels with her. 'Here, catch this,' (throws down box of ducats to Lorenzo), 'I'm going back to get some more.'

And Lorenzo? That will keep him happy. He can't believe his luck. He won't be able to back out after that. He needs it too much. Off they go on a trans-European spree (last seen disappearing in a gondola in the direction of Genoa). Spend like there's no tomorrow. Eighty ducats on a meal, swap a priceless ring given to Shylock by his wife for a monkey. The insouciance, the frivolity of it all. Bassanio and Gratiano give away their rings without a third thought. Shylock would not part with his for 'a wilderness of monkeys'. But here the ring is reduced to the level of a cheap bauble for a cheap thrill. Buying the moment. Living in the present. A nasty bit of work, Jessica. Some may say a chip off the old block. But we see no evidence in Shylock's relationship with her that he deserves such treatment. Certainly her betrayal of faith and family and her robbing Shylock of his wealth contribute mightily to Shylock's desire for revenge on the whole pack of

Christians. Lorenzo's act of stealing Jessica away becomes a symbol for the whole decadent behaviour of Antonio and friends, and Antonio's forcing Shylock to become a Christian is a punishment worse than any loss of wealth.

Launcelot Gobbo calls Shylock a devil. Yet apart from telling us that Launcelot eats a lot and is lazy (possibly true), Shylock treats Launcelot more with resignation than anger. He even discusses Launcelot's defection from his service with Bassanio.

> **BASSANIO: Shylock thy master spoke with me this day,**
> **And hath preferred thee . . .**
>
> (Act II, Scene ii)

All seems to be amicable between them; Launcelot even admits that he has a bad conscience, that it is the Devil himself urging him to leave Shylock. Reason? Bassanio has come into money (Antonio's) and is hiring men at a good rate, poaching them, and giving them flash uniforms (to impress). It's called bettering oneself, trading up. Just as Jessica destroys Shylock with her betrayal, so Launcelot Gobbo reduces his father to tears of despair with a cruel trick, unleashing in his sand-blind father a passion of grief that he had not bargained for, by pretending to be dead. Yet another of Shakespeare's clown/nobility parallels, this one involving offspring.

> **LAUNCELOT: Ergo, Master Launcelot . . . is indeed deceased,**
> **or as you would say in plain terms, gone to heaven.**
> **GOBBO: Marry, God forbid! The boy was the very staff of my**
> **age, my very prop.**
>
> (Act II, Scene ii)

Thus do Christians play so lightly with emotions. Life and death, marriage and money are jokes, oaths are to be broken and parents laughed at.

* * *

And so to Shylock.

All right, so he is careful with his money. Usury was frowned on in Elizabethan society. For us it is par for the course. We call them banks. They bleed us dry for profit. The twenty-first century pound of flesh is negative equity, exorbitant interest rates, repossession. Shylock would have been in good company with Barclays, NatWest and others and Antonio with Enron. Shylock hates Antonio because he is a Christian – more, because he lends out money gratis. Antonio hates Shylock because he is a Jew – more, because he lends out money for profit, thus breaking up the cartel, the gentleman's club.

However, Shylock is not a gambler. Antonio is. So what makes Shylock gamble on what has to be a very long shot? What are the chances of *none* of Antonio's ships coming back before three months have elapsed? After all he sent them out to the four corners of the globe, covering his options.

ANTONIO: My ventures are not in one bottom trusted,
Nor to one place; nor is my whole estate
Upon the fortune of this present year.

(Act I, Scene i)

SHYLOCK: . . . He hath an argosy bound to Tripolis, another
to the Indies; . . . a third at Mexico, a fourth for England, and
other ventures he hath squandered abroad.

(Act I, Scene iii)

He hasn't put all his eggs in one argosy. He expects them *all* back within two months. Shylock cannot have expected the bond ever to be forfeit. It's like backing the outsider at the Grand National at a thousand to one. Or playing Lotto. But of course, he can't charge Antonio interest. That would be playing into the Christian's hands. He has to be bigger than that. He devises a method which he calls 'a merry sport'. Is it that? 'If I can catch him once upon the hip . . .' Yet it can hardly be serious. Even when he gets the news that Antonio has possibly lost a ship, his first thought is that he might not get his money back, not that he'll get his pound of flesh.

79

> **SHYLOCK: There I have another bad match! A bankrupt, a prodigal, who dares scarce show his head on the Rialto, a beggar that was used to come so smug upon the mart!**
>
> (Act III, Scene i)

The situation only turns real after Jessica's defection, spurred on by the unbelievable chance that all the ships have indeed been lost at sea. Or have they? Where did Portia get the letter which she produces back in Belmont that tells him that some of his boats have safely come to harbour? How long had she had it? Has she known all along? Is it possible that both Shylock and Antonio have been put through the mill needlessly?

> **PORTIA: . . . you shall not know by what strange accident I chancèd on this letter.**
>
> (Act V, Scene i)

The quality of Portia's mercy may well indeed have been strained if this is the case. Merciless would then be a better description of her handling of the situation.

The play is finely balanced between disgust at Shylock's insistence on exacting his pound of flesh and disgust at the racism that has brought him to it. Yet he has two speeches that in any context could be seen as a plea for racial tolerance and equality.

> **SHYLOCK: . . . Hath not a Jew eyes? Hath not a Jew hands, organs, dimensions, senses, affections, passions? Fed with the same food, hurt with the same weapons, subject to the same diseases, healed by the same means, warmed and cooled by the same winter and summer as a Christian is? If you prick us, do we not bleed? If you tickle us, do we not laugh? And if you poison us, do we not die? And if you wrong us, shall we not revenge? . . .**
>
> (Act III, Scene i)

The speech finishes with the key line that defines the whole rationale behind Shylock's revenge: 'The villainy you teach me I will execute, and it shall go hard but I will better the instruction.' Shylock's bloodthirsty act is not simply the result of the way the Venetians have treated him but an exact replica of Christian values. His cruelty will mirror theirs. In the eyes of the law he is 'doing no wrong'.

> **SHYLOCK: You have among you many a purchased slave,**
> **Which like your asses and your dogs and mules**
> **You use in abject and in slavish parts,**
> **Because you bought them. Shall I say to you,**
> **'Let them be free! Marry them to your heirs!**
> **Why sweat they under burdens? . . .'**
>   . . . . .
>   **You will answer,**
> **'The slaves are ours.' So do I answer you.**
> **The pound of flesh which I demand of him**
> **Is dearly bought, 'tis mine, and I will have it.**
> **If you deny me, fie upon your law!**
>
>   **(Act IV, Scene i)**

Here Shylock shows a clinical insight into the mercenary motives of Christian Venetian behaviour. He speculates with money, they speculate with lives and goods. He tries to join them and is defeated. There are too many of them and they are better at the game than he is. The lesson is, don't try and step over the class/race divide – they'll beat you every time. And as Shylock trails off into the sunset – stripped of his wealth, his faith, his hearth and home, that is the last we see of him. Yet there is still more flesh to be extracted.

* * *

And so to Belmont. They come from all corners to try and guess which casket contains Portia's portrait. It is like trying to guess the weight of the ram at the village fair. Rather like Bianca in *The Taming of the Shrew* – will it be the octogenarian Gremio or the young Tranio bartering for her hand who'll win her? For Portia it's touch and go. Will it be the German drunk or the English idiot? Life and love are a lottery. Try and put them off – make them sign a piece of paper swearing that if they choose wrongly they will never marry. It works with some. Never mind that it is impossible to enforce – it's the thought that does it. Dad certainly knew what he was doing. If anybody is going to get the wealth that he has left behind, at least make them sweat for it. Presumably Portia was too young to wed when he was alive or he would have sorted it all out before he popped off.

So choose. Gold. Silver. Lead. Marriages are a convenience, a cementing of property and fortunes. Love plays no part. So who composed the rhymes to go in the caskets? Who thought up the effigies – skull and puppet – to go inside the gold and silver, cruelly mocking the choosers? Die – loser! Who chose lead as the one in which to place the portrait – the least alluring? What must Portia feel as Morocco and Arragon are contemplating the choice? It's crucial that Bassanio chooses right. Do they help him (Cough – n-o-o-o! After all there's more than a million at stake.) Daddy obviously didn't want some gold-digger frittering away his fortune and it could so easily have been some wealthy prince or potentate not put off by some sworn unenforceable oath. But he reckoned without Bassanio's cunning. *Faute de mieux*, Portia ends up with the biggest chancer of the lot, a crow with feathers painted green. The gambler, not even waiting to suss out the lie of the land, all the chips on one number, pulls it off. The hard-bitten bitch of an heiress gets the footloose and fancy free buccaneer. It's a marriage made in lead.

Three marriages, three recipes for disaster. Against the backdrop of a moon going in and out of the clouds, now light now dark, we get the feeling that all is not exactly roses between Jessica and Lorenzo.

> **LORENZO: The moon shines bright. In such a night as this,**
> **When the sweet wind did gently kiss the trees**
> **And they did make no noise, in such a night**
> **Troilus methinks mounted the Troyan walls,**
> **And sighed his soul toward the Grecian tents**
> **Where Cressid lay that night.**

JESSICA: In such a night
Did Thisbe fearfully o'ertrip the dew,
And saw the lion's shadow ere himself,
And ran dismayed away.
LORENZO: In such a night
Stood Dido with a willow in her hand
Upon the wild sea banks, and waft her love
To come again to Carthage.
JESSICA: In such a night
Medea gathered the enchanted herbs
That did renew old Aeson.
LORENZO: In such a night
Did Jessica steal from the wealthy Jew,
And with an unthrift love did run from Venice
As far as Belmont.
JESSICA: In such a night
Did young Lorenzo swear he loved her well,
Stealing her soul with many vows of faith,
And ne'er a true one.
LORENZO: In such a night
Did pretty Jessica, like a little shrew,
Slander her love, and he forgave it her.
JESSICA: I would out-night you, did nobody come;
But hark, I hear the footing of a man.

                                       (Act V, Scene i)

No playful banter this, it is a no-holds-barred battle of the sexes, the classical allusions hardly masking the full-blown row into which it is about to degenerate when interrupted by the arrival of a messenger. Jessica will not be mollified even by music. Portia arrives back, her mood bitter and acerbic. The music also turns her off.

PORTIA: . . . Methinks it sounds much sweeter than by day
         . . . . .
The crow doth sing as sweetly as the lark
When neither is attended, and I think
The nightingale, if she should sing by day
When every goose is cackling, would be thought

No better a musician than the wren.
How many things by season seasoned are
To their right praise and true perfection!
Peace! . . .

(Act V, Scene i)

Out of nothing a row erupts between Nerissa and Gratiano. It's those rings. Gratiano is damned if he is going to carry the can all on his own. He fingers Bassanio. No honour among friends. The women twist the knife. Once again Portia shows no mercy. No comic scene this. A deadly earnest extraction of a metaphorical pound of flesh.

PORTIA: If you had known the virtue of the ring,
Or half her worthiness that gave the ring,
Or your own honour to contain the ring,
You would not then have parted with the ring.

(Act V, Scene i)

Antonio is silent. And is silent. Until finally he is forced to intervene and admit that the ring was given away on his behalf and in a rush of blood to the head pledges an oath once again on behalf of his friend:

ANTONIO: I once did lend my body for his wealth,
Which but for him that had your husband's ring
Had quite miscarried. I dare be bound again,
My soul upon the forfeit, that your lord
Will never more break faith advisedly.

(Act V, Scene i)

Will he never learn? He was almost fatally wrong once. He could be so again. There is nothing in Bassanio's past or personality that says he will stay true to Portia. It obviously hurts Antonio to deal with this lady who is now legitimately Bassanio's wife, his rival for Bassanio's affections. He needn't have worried – Portia has Bassanio wriggling on a hook and intends to keep him there for the rest of his life. Lorenzo's boat too comes home (what did he do to deserve it?).

NERISSA: There do I give to you and Jessica
From the rich Jew, a special deed of gift,
After his death, of all he dies possessed of.
LORENZO: Fair ladies, you drop manna in the way
Of starvèd people.

(Act V, Scene i)

What happened to the monkey?

Gratiano rounds off a bad night's work with a few dirty jokes about keeping safe Nerissa's 'ring'. And Shylock? He has probably committed suicide. They're a nasty lot on the Rialto.

The Winter's Tale

bohemian rhapsody - pulling the wool

'In the bleak midwinter . . .'

Modern analysis of this beautiful play has concentrated on Hermione's resurrection in an attempt to rationalise what appears to be a Christian 'miracle'. For many commentators *The Winter's Tale* (not *A Winter's Tale,* notice) is also a fairy tale. Reporting the reunion of Leontes and Perdita a courtier comments, 'This news, which is called true, is so like an old tale that the verity of it is in strong suspicion. (Act V, Scene ii). In Act V, Scene iii when Hermione *'comes to life'* Paulina cynically observes:

> **That she is living,**
> **Were it but told you, should be hooted at**
> **Like an old tale.**

The Old Shepherd on finding a box of gold immediately believes it to be 'fairy gold'. Time and again we are reminded of the fantastical nature of events. And yet, as is so often the case with Shakespeare, these supernatural events are entirely explicable, the characters' gullibility mirroring the audience's desire to suspend disbelief and enter into the theatre world of make-belive. After all, we don't want the theatre to be like real life do we? We all want to believe in something don't we? Please don't spoil the story, daddy.

For Hermione's resurrection is a con. In collusion with Paulina she has kept herself hidden away for sixteen years waiting for Perdita's return.

> **HERMIONE:** . . . For thou shalt hear that I,
> **Knowing by Paulina that the oracle**
> **Gave hope thou wast in being, have preserved**
> **Myself to see the issue.**
>
> (Act V, Scene iii)

The 'miraculous' denouement poses more questions than it answers.

> **MAMILLIUS: A sad tale's best for winter. . . .**
> . . . . .
> **There was a man – . . .**
> **Dwelt by a churchyard – I will tell it softly:**
> **Yond crickets shall not hear it.**
>
> (Act II, Scene i)

And not only is this tale told softly, it is so soft that unless you listen carefully you can hardly hear it. . . .

The condition:

> **OFFICER: Hermione, Queen to the worthy Leontes, King of Sicilia, thou art here accused and arraigned of high treason, in committing adultery with Polixenes, King of Bohemia, and conspiring with Camillo to take away the life of our sovereign lord the King, thy royal husband; the pretence whereof being by circumstances partly laid open, thou, Hermione, contrary to the faith and allegiance of a true subject, didst counsel and aid them, for their better safety, to fly away by night.**

A Shakespeare tale never begins at the beginning. Just as winter is half-way between summer and spring, so we enter the tale of Leontes's jealousy slap bang in the middle. *The Winter's Tale* almost begins where *Othello* leaves off. 'Unmotivated', 'senseless', 'groundless', 'no cause', run the condemnatory phrases of his jealousy. Unmotivated? We soon learn that Hermione is heavily pregnant, and that Polixenes's stay in Sicilia has been nine months:

> **POLIXINES: Nine changes of the watery star hath been**
> **The shepherd's note since we have left our throne**
> **Without a burden.**
>
> (Act I, Scene ii)

Nine months – a chance length of time? What has the King of Bohemia been doing away from his country for nine months? And what about his son, some seven or eight years old? He hasn't seen his Dad in all that time. And how does Polixenes view him?

> **POLIXENES: He's all my exercise, my mirth, my matter;**
> **Now my sworn friend, and then mine enemy;**
> **My parasite, my soldier, statesman, all.**
> **He makes a July's day short as December,**
> **And with his varying childness cures in me**
> **Thoughts that would thick my blood.**
>
> (Act I, Scene ii)

If Polixenes loves his son all that much why has he been hanging around Sicilia so long? Has he a wife? If not, his son has had neither mother nor father around him at a critical age. If yes, then he has been away from both wife and son for an unconscionable amount of time. How has he occupied himself? Leontes would have been busy with the affairs of state, for he obviously runs a tight ship. Polixenes would have been thrown back on the company of the queen.

We learn that as lads Polixenes and Leontes hunted the lasses together. There's even the hint of a Hermione/Polixenes/his wife-to-be threesome and the news that Polixenes has put it about a bit.

POLIXENES: . . . Oh my most sacred lady,
Temptations have since then been born to's: for
In those unfledged days was my wife a girl;
Your precious self had not then crossed the eyes
Of my young playfellow.
HERMIONE: Grace to boot!
Of this make no conclusion, lest you say
Your queen and I are devils. Yet go on:
Th'offences we have made you do we'll answer,
If you first sinned with us, and that with us
You did continue fault, and that you slipped not
With any but with us.

(Act I, Scene ii)

Seems grounds enough for jealousy to me. And once the imagination is running riot, every gesture is misinterpreted. But no smoke without fire. Only if Hermione's behaviour can be misinterpreted, can Leontes's jealousy be justified.

LEONTES: Is whispering nothing?
Is leaning cheek to cheek? Is meeting noses?
Kissing with inside lip? Stopping the career
Of laughter with a sigh? – a note infallible
Of breaking honesty. Horsing foot on foot?
Skulking in corners? Wishing clocks more swift?
Hours minutes? Noon midnight? And all eyes
Blind with the pin and web but theirs, theirs only,
That would unseen be wicked – is this nothing?
Why, then the world and all that's in't is nothing;
The sky covering is nothing; Bohemia nothing;
My wife is nothing; nor nothing have these nothings,
If this be nothing.

(Act I, Scene ii)

Do we believe this or is Leontes now so far gone that it is pure invention? Hermione flirts, so much is clear. Playing with fire. Perhaps the fact that she is eight months pregnant gives her a sense of security that makes her dare to push the envelope of sexual banter and behaviour further than she would otherwise contemplate. She looks her best and knows it. Having stayed so long, why doesn't Polixenes wait to celebrate the birth of his best friend's child? It could be his – maybe he doesn't want to stay around to spot the likeness . . .

* * *

We learn three things from the opening scene with Camillo and Archidamus. One, that Sicilia and Bohemia are totally different societies – the same contrasts that exist between Scandinavian and Mediterranean cultures. (Never mind that in Shakespeare's world Bohemia has a shoreline and Sicilia is more associated with puritanism and austerity than sun and sand.) In Sicilia the trains run on time. In Bohemia it's mañana. Two, that Polixenes and Leontes are best friends from childhood; that a bond exists between them that nothing will ever tear asunder. (Therefore we know immediately that the story will show just how that rift occurs.) Three, that the boy Mamillius is the great hope of the nation (so something is going to happen to him). The ground rules are clearly laid out and Leontes's paranoia precipitates all that follows.

This is an autocratic society. What the king says goes. Off with his (her) head. The fire raging in his heart leads him to excess. His belief that Polixenes has fathered his child causes him to demand its incineration, commuted to the 'lesser' punishment of being left in a wild and remote place:

> **LEONTES:** . . . **This brat is none of mine:**
> **It is the issue of Polixenes.**
> **Hence with it, and together with the dam**
> **Commit them to the fire!**
>
> **(Act II, Scene iii)**

Magnanimously he orders independent proof, smug in the knowledge that he is right:

> LEONTES: Yet, for a greater confirmation –
> For in an act of this importance 'twere
> Most piteous to be wild – I have dispatched in post
> To sacred Delphos, to Apollo's temple,
> Cleomenes and Dion, whom you know
> Of stuffed sufficiency. Now from the oracle
> They will bring all; whose spiritual counsel, had,
> Shall stop or spur me. Have I done well?

> (Act II, Scene i)

The second resolution on Iraq. We'll go to the UN if that will satisfy you, but it won't make any difference – we're going to war anyway.

In a play that mixes the pagan with the Christian, the oracle is a given. Where all else is supposition, Apollo must be believed. It exonerates all concerned. This is the only truth, for elsewhere in this play nothing is what it seems. Deception, self or otherwise, is endemic. Only the oracle does not deceive.

Let us look at the deception list.

Leontes: himself

Camillo: Leontes, Polixenes, Florizel and Perdita

Hermione: the world

Polixenes: Leontes, his subjects, his son

Paulina: the world, particularly Leontes

Florizel: his father, the village community, Leontes (she comes from Libya, lies Florizel to Leontes, I bring my father's greetings, etc.)

Perdita: her father, her brother, the village, Leontes

Old Shepherd: the entire parish

His son: ditto

Autolycus: everybody. Note however the honesty with which Autolycus – 'My revenue is the silly cheat . . . For the life to come, I sleep out the thought of it' – claims to do it.

AUTOLYCUS: The Prince himself is about a piece of iniquity – stealing away from his father, with his clog at his heels. If I thought it were a piece of honesty to acquaint the King withal, I would not do't. I hold it the more knavery to conceal it; and therein am I constant to my profession.

(Act IV, Scene iv)

He deceives to survive, makes no bones about it. Everyone else is practising deception, they would say, in the name of their own and others' good. Parallel scenes of honest roguery and self-righteous nobility are common in Shakespeare. The Duke in *Measure for Measure* has just procured Mariana to sleep undetected with Angelo in place of the Novice Isabella, when he runs into the pimp Pompey and begins to froth at mouth: 'Fie sir, a filthy bawd!' He then throws him in jail for living off immoral earnings. It is all right for the Duke to procure sex covertly but not for Pompey to ply his 'legitimate' trade. Double standards. One rule for the rich, another for the poor. So while the nobs deceive in defence of self-righteous behaviour, Autolycus risks hanging for picking pockets. One person only, Antigonus, isn't into deception, but he gets torn to pieces by a bear for his pains.

Camillo, from humble beginnings – 'Leontes, whom I from meaner form / Have benched and reared to worship' – rises to be Leontes's right-hand man and most trusted adviser, deceives him into thinking he will poison Polixenes – swears an oath indeed – and then heads off with Polixenes to Bohemia. Canny, a machiavellian survivor, he weighs up all the odds, susses out all the options:

CAMILLO: . . . But for me,
What case stand I in? I must be the poisoner
Of good Polixenes, and my ground to do't
Is the obedience to a master – one
Who, in rebellion with himself, will have
All that are his so too. To do this deed,
Promotion follows. If I could find example
Of thousands that had struck anointed kings
And flourished after, I'd not do't; but since
Nor brass, nor stone, nor parchment bears not one,

> Let villainy itself forswear't. I must
> Forsake the court: to do't or no is certain
> To me a break-neck.
>
> (Act I, Scene ii)

Sixteen years later, in Bohemia, he has worked himself into the same position with Polixenes:

> **POLIXENES: As thou lov'st me, Camillo, wipe not out the rest of thy services by leaving me now. The need I have of thee thine own goodness hath made. Better not to have had thee than thus to want thee. Thou, having made me businesses which none without thee can sufficiently manage, must either stay to execute them thyself or take away with thee the very services thou hast done . . .**
>
> (Act IV, Scene ii)

But the positions are now reversed, Leontes back home repenting and in mourning, Polixenes in Bohemia autocratic and laying a heavy scene on Camillo and his son, the Old Shepherd and Perdita. There is a distinct parallel between the tyrannical behaviour and language of Leontes when ordering Antigonus to do away with the baby:

> Thou, traitor, hast set on thy wife to this.
> My child? Away with't! . . .
>   . . . take it hence
> And see it instantly consumed with fire:
>   . . . Take it up straight!
> Within this hour bring me word tis done,
>   . . . or I'll seize thy life,
> With what thou else call'st thine. If thou refuse,
> And wil't encounter with my wrath, say so:
> The bastard brains with these my proper hands
> Shall I dash out. . . .
>
> (Act II, Scene iii)

and the dire threats of death and torture that Polexenes utters to the

Old Shepherd and his daughter:

> . . . Thou, old traitor,
> I am sorry that by hanging thee I can
> But shorten thy life one week. – And thou, fresh piece
> Of excellent witchcraft, . . .
>
> . . . . .
>
> I'll have thy beauty scratched with briars and made
> More homely than thy state. . . .
>
> . . . . .
>
> These rural latches to his entrance open,
> Or hoop his body more with thy embraces,
> I will devise a death as cruel for thee
> As thou art tender to't.

(Act IV, Scene iv)

This is the second time that Perdita suffers such horrific threats – once as a baby and once as a teenager. There is more than an echo here of *The Tempest* and Prospero's dire threats to Ferdinand if he takes Miranda's virginity before they are married, a reminder that William was not above a bit of recycling if it suited his purpose. For Perdita it means that for a second time in her life, not of her own choosing, she will be at the mercy of the high seas as she tries to escape with Florizel.

So, if Camillo wants to get back to Sicilia it's time for him to deceive Polixenes. He uses the escape of the two kids to furnish his own needs and instantly betrays them, persuades them to make for Sicilia.

> CAMILLO: What I do next shall be to tell the King
> Of this escape and whither they are bound;
> Wherein my hope is I shall so prevail
> To force him after: in whose company
> I shall re-view Sicilia, for whose sight
> I have a woman's longing.

(Act IV, Scene iv)

Which means of course that when Polexenes catches up with them in Sicilia, it will be the chop for the Old Shepherd and his son, a nunnery at best for Perdita (minus scratched out eyes) and a chain round his ankle (literally and metaphorically) for Florizel for the rest of his life. But none of this matters to Camillo - he's back in his beloved Sicilia. To hell with the rest. He deserves his marriage to Paulina (what a surprise) at the end of the play, perhaps Leontes's retrospective punishment for leaving him all those years ago, and for Paulina's sixteen-year deception?

* * *

Bohemia. A Romany community? New Age travellers? A hippy compound? Arcadian nymphs and shepherds? The Bagwam, a maharishi? Pot-smoking, opium-filling, laid back, let it all hang out, communal living? Many interpretations are based on Achidamus's description:

ARCHDAMUS: . . . We will give you sleepy drinks, that your senses, unintelligent of our insufficience, may, though they cannot praise us, as little accuse us.

(Act I, Scene i)

The truth is much nearer home, for what Shakespeare is describing is rural Warwickshire. In Polixenes's very first lines there is a mention of shepherds. We go from the austerity and sterility of the Sicilian court to the celebration at the end of shearing time in Bohemia. Shearing is hard. I know. I've done it. Two or three hundred times a day (not me, I hasten to add) wrestling with a hundredweight of sheep and wool, turning, twisting, shearing. It's communal and traditional. As long as there are sheep they have to be shorn, and for many farms shearing has been on the same day or days each year for centuries. In the days of hand shears the community moved from one farm to the next, the children rolling the wool and sweeping, the women rolling and cooking. The entire village would have spent several days at the Old Shepherd's farm, now the largest in the district thanks to the 'fairy gold' found with Perdita, and at the end of it all would celebrate. The hard work is over — eat, drink and be merry.

This is not about shepherdesses in frilly dresses or tipis and yurts. This is about 'hard-handed men' (and women) and a community binding round itself, ensuring its survival through the common work ethic, the antithesis of the court life of Sicilia. No Arcadian, Victorian, pastoral scene this, no tables groaning with pies and beef.

The transition from Sicilia to Bohemia is a symbolic one. And, just as winter must recede and spring and summer follow, so the sheep must shed their wool and the lightness and freedom that they experience after the heaviness and weight of the wool parallel the retreat of winter. Yet even here the dead weight of autocracy can descend. Liberal, sunny, free-living Bohemia feels the tyrannical hand of the king reach out to grip the Old Shepherd by the throat. There has been a hint of this conservatism on the part of Polixenes earlier in his treatment of Camillo: 'Of that fatal country, Sicilia, I prithee speak no more.' I'm not letting you go back.

Now he lays the Capulet/Juliet scene on his son Florizel. This is unusual in Shakespeare in that customarily the girls are forbidden to marry their choice. But rather like Hamlet, Florizel is not allowed to 'carve for himself'. What a bit of luck that Perdita turns out to be a princess, eh? Leontes and Polixenes have now reversed positions. Would Leontes have interceded on Florizel's behalf? Probably. Would Polixenes have listened? Probably not.

* * *

Nature or nurture? Is there any basis for genes dominating environment? Genetically Perdita will certainly have inherited her family's physical characteristics, but all her upbringing has been at the hands of the Old Shepherd and his son. How old was the son when Perdita was found? Seven, eight — the same age as Mamillius and Polixenes's boy? Or about seventeen or eighteen? If the latter then he is at least thirty-four when Perdita reigns as queen of the feast. The mother is dead.

> SHEPHERD: Fie, daughter! When my old wife lived, upon
> This day she was both pantler, butler, cook;
> Both dame and servant; welcomed all, served all;
> Would sing her song and dance her turn; now here,
> At upper end o'th'table, now i'th'middle;
> On his shoulder, and his; her face o'fire
> With labour, and the thing she took to quench it:
> She would to each one sip. You are retired,
> As if you were a feasted one and not
> The hostess of the meeting.

> (Act IV, Scene iv)

Presumably Perdita has been brought up in a male household, cared for by a wet-nurse hired with the gold found in the chest. The Shepherd, with his new-found wealth, careful though he would have had to be, would have put it about a bit. Farm-hands, helpers – certainly the Shepherd would have been at pains to ensure that Perdita has had the very best of care in order not to offend the 'fairies'. Read, write, sew, sing? All the accomplishments of a young lady. These are not innate – they are acquired. But something else is acquired too. A sense of value, of place, of community. Perdita would have helped in the house, around the farm; would know all about animals, the seasons, the countryside, wild flowers:

> PERDITA: . . . Here's flowers for you:
> Hot lavender, mints, savory, marjoram;
> The marigold, that goes to bed with' sun
> And with him rises weeping; these are flowers
> Of middle summer, and I think they are given
> To men of middle age.

> (Act IV, Scene iv)

She is unaccustomed to dressing up in anything other than everyday working clothes, disproving the theory that all girls love frilly dresses, and despises the outward show of something she is not: 'Most goddess-like pranked up' . . . 'in these my borrowed flaunts'. She hates affectation:

**PERDITA: Methinks I play as I have seen them do
In Whitsun pastorals: sure this robe of mine
Does change my disposition.**

(Act IV, Scene iv)

These values are those of an unpretentious rural community at one with itself. She will carry them with her to the Sicilian court, along with her accent. (Rural. How broad?)

It is these values that Florizel falls in love with.

The Old Shepherd must have indulged in a fair bit of subterfuge to keep his secret. Did he ever bother to find out whose baby Perdita was? What yarn did he spin his neighbours? Did he say that he had found the baby, or did he pass it off as the illegitimate and unwanted offspring of some distant rich relative that he had taken in out of pity? Perdita never for one moment thinks that she is anything other than the legitimate daughter of the Shepherd. What happened to her mother? Did she die in childbirth or when Perdita was too young to remember? Another story to sort out for the folks next door. Sixteen years ago the Old Shepherd and his son obviously couldn't read or they would have known from Antigonus's letters who she was. Or is it that they kept the secret to themselves? How else would they have known that her name was Perdita? But the story hinges on their belief that Perdita is a changeling, so they cannot have read the letters.

* * *

How does Perdita feel about suddenly finding out that her real mother and father are a king and queen? Will she change? A fair old shock to the system, really, to find out that, far from inheriting a few chunks of your mother's old furniture, you're in line to land up owning two countries. Could this be the retrospective reward for the Old Shepherd's humanity? Maybe old Will believed in fairies after all.

Hoops to jump through everywhere. How many did Hermione and Paulina have to jump through to disguise the continuing existence of Hermione? Leontes defies the oracle, and instantly receives the news that his son has died. Hermione collapses – 'Look down and see what death is doing!' – and is carried out. Paulina comes back in and announces that Hermione is indeed dead. Leontes asks to be taken to her and view the dead body.

Questions abound:

(a) Is Paulina already pretending?

(b) Has she cooked up the survival plan with Hermione in the short interval between Hermione being carried off and Paulina's return?

(c) Does Paulina genuinely believe that Hermione is dead – some death-like faint, just like Juliet, that causes her to be buried alive and then hammer on the coffin at a later point to be let out? If so, who lets her out? There must have been a funeral so –

(d) Was a body substituted?

(e) Was the coffin empty?

(f) Was Hermione in it and let out by Paulina?

(g) and (h) Who knew and colluded in what part of the charade?

Hermione is secreted away for sixteen years, growing older in the process.

> **LEONTES: [of the statue] . . . But yet, Paulina,**
> **Hermione was not so much wrinkled, nothing**
> **So agèd as this seems.**
>
> (Act V, Scene iii)

Fed in secret, exercising in secret, waiting for the moment when Perdita would return. There is to be no miraculous resurrection; the statue trick is a cold, careful, calculated plan. Deception as an art form. A huge con trick posing as a miracle. The clues are there from the moment that Antigonus goes off with the baby to Bohemia.

In his dream Hermione comes to him on board the boat. He jumps to all the wrong conclusions:

ANTIGONUS: . . . Dreams are toys:
Yet for this once, yea superstitiously,
I will be squared by this. I do believe
Hermione hath suffered death, and that
Apollo would, this being indeed the issue
Of King Polixenes, it should here be laid,
Either for life or death, upon the earth
Of its right father.

(Act III, Scene iii)

The baby is not Polixenes's —we know that from the oracle (and the oracle never lies). Therefore the conclusion that Hermione is dead is also false.

Sixteen years later with the pressure growing on the king to produce an heir (failure to provide for the succession breeds civil war and chaos), Paulina makes Leontes swear never to marry:

PAULINA: Will you swear
Never to marry but by my free leave?

. . . . .
Unless another,
As like Hermione as is her picture,
Affront his eye.

(Act V, Scene i)

As Paulina is unaware at this moment of the existence of Perdita, the inference is obvious. Anyway Perdita is Leontes's daughter, although it is clear when he finds out that she is not married that he fancies her something rotten.

PAULINA: Sir, my liege,
Your eye hath too much youth in't!

(Act V, Scene i)

Paulina knows that the time is fast approaching when the game will be up. She will not be able to hold off the heir-seeking court jackals much longer. After the revelations of Perdita's identity, comes the news of the statue carved in Hermione's likeness. Of course no one is allowed to touch it. The 'statue' comes alive. Shock, horror, not a dry eye in the house. The penny drops:

> **LEONTES:**   **. . . for I saw her,**
> **As I thought, dead; and have in vain**
> **Said many a prayer upon her grave.**
>
>   **(Act V, Scene iii)**

Do you mean I have been on my knees for sixteen years for nothing? The deception boomerangs back.

What lessons have been learned? Polixenes has been let off the hook; he doesn't have to make a choice. Leontes is miffed that no one told him about Hermione and is throwing his weight around again. Hermione says not a word to Leontes in the last scene, pre-occupied as she is with Perdita. But that silence is eloquent. Is she going to forgive Leontes for causing her to be incarcerated for sixteen years, for leaving her baby in the wilds (what a bit of luck it was found, eh?), for bringing about the death of her son? Is the winter over for the man who dwelt by a churchyard? Questions.

Macbeth

the Scottish play – dealing with the English

Macbeth is known in theatrical circles as 'the Scottish play'. It is strange that this unconscious acknowledgement of the Celtic origins of the play about the struggle for the soul of Scotland is rarely reflected in production – give or take a kilt and a caber or two.

For this is a play about Scotland caught at a time of political transition. The battleground may be rooted historically in the Scotland of 1100, but the political action is firmly in James VI and I's English court. So how has the play come to be seen down the ages as the conflict of good and evil, with good (of course) triumphing in true pantomime tradition? Nowhere is this reflected more strongly than in the old stage superstition that even to mention the play by its title would be to bring down untold misfortune on the production, the theatre, the audience – the whole world – at the single utterance of that dreaded name. This ignores the fact that there are probably more accidents associated with the duel in *Hamlet,* or Juliets down the ages falling off the balcony, than any in *Macbeth*. So – The Scottish Play.

In his Introduction to the Arden edition of *Macbeth* Kenneth Muir cites with ideological certainty a number of conservative analyses of the play. It is 'a statement of evil'; 'a picture of a special battle in a universal war and the battleground is in the soul of Macbeth and his wife'; 'Shakespeare's most profound and mature vision of evil'; 'the whole play may be writ down as a wrestling of destruction with creation'; 'the contrast between light and darkness is part of the general antithesis between good and evil, devil and angels, evil and grace, hell and heaven'.

What examining board could resist such an inviting Christian analysis? With such deeply entrenched conservative views as a benchmark for study, what pupil would dare challenge such authoritative assumptions? For the problem that arises with the use of the word evil is one of metaphysical subjectivity. What is 'evil'? How do you define it? *Who* defines it? It is an abstract, dependant on a Christian theology that posits an opposite force in Satan and Mephistopheles.

Macbeth is not a man driven to extremes by forces of darkness beyond his control. He is the ultimate existentialist, someone for whom the awakening of the realisation that he alone is responsible for his actions leads to Shakespeare's most definitive existential statement of the nihilism of power, the astonishing

> Tomorrow, and tomorrow, and tomorrow,
> Creeps in this petty pace from day to day
> To the last syllable of recorded time;
> And all our yesterdays have lighted fools
> The way to dusty death. Out, out, brief candle!
> Life's but a walking shadow, a poor player
> That struts and frets his hour upon the stage,
> And then is heard no more. It is a tale
> Told by an idiot, full of sound and fury,
> Signifying nothing.
>
> (Act V, Scene v)

This is the creed of ruthless individualism, someone for whose 'own good / All causes shall give way' (Act III, Scene iv), a modern creed that strikes a resonant chord with generations of Thatcher's children.

So what kind of Scotland is left behind after his demise? What deal did Malcolm do with the English king to get the loan of ten thousand troops?

> . . . before thy here-approach,
> Old Seyward with ten thousand war-like men,
> Already at a point, was setting forth.
>
> (Act IV, Scene iii)

Ten thousand is worth a million now. And there is no country in the world that would take part in such an invasion without doing some kind of *quid pro quo* deal that involves the carving up of the country that it is invading. Witness the desperate attempt of Bush and the assembled might of the US Right to bribe and coerce other nations into helping it invade Iraq with promises of billions of aid. Malcolm has sold Scotland down the line in order to secure his throne – there is no way back from a deal that carves Scotland up with the English.

> MALCOLM: . . . My thanes and kinsmen,
> Henceforth be earls, the first that ever Scotland
> In such an honour named.
>
> (Act V, Scene vi)

Note the invisible bullet, the thanes, the chiefs of the clans, the leaders of Scottish society are to be transformed into earls, Anglicised, colonised, the passing of an era. 'Fair is foul and foul is fair'. This is the moment that prefigures the rule of Scotland from Westminster, the court of James VI and I. It is Malcolm's final speech that sets him apart from his predecessors and most clearly marks the transition of Scotland from a feudal power to a subservient colony.

For Malcolm is the apotheosis of *Realpolitik:* Malcolm the materialist; Malcolm the politician; Malcolm, like Prince John in *Henry IV* Part Two, heralding a new era of ruthless, pragmatic government. What is his reaction on being present when Macduff receives the news of the slaughter of his family?

> Be this the whetstone of your sword; let grief
> Convert to anger; blunt not the heart, enrage it.
>
> (Act IV, Scene iii)

Use it, Macduff, use it!

Malcolm seizes with alacrity the opportunity offered him on a plate. Here's the perfect guy to do the work of sorting out Macbeth for him. Macduff's consuming desire for revenge makes him the ideal weapon of mass destruction. Malcolm can send him in to do battle against Macbeth without having to put himself anywhere near the front line. Then walk in and claim the victory. What a shit.

As the play begins so the play ends – with conquerors high on bloodletting. Macduff has beaten Macbeth in an old, one-to-one, hand-to-hand, heroic duel. Macduff, concerned only with personal revenge, does the dirty work. Malcolm, without having to fight, picks up the crown, Macduff merely a means to an imperial end, a conduit through which Malcolm could vanquish his foe. But technically Malcolm himself is a usurper. Although 'named', he renounced the title and fled to England. Macbeth was then 'named' by the thanes and therefore ruled legitimately, albeit having ascended by illegitimate means.

And what sort of Scotland will it be? Macduff the 'patriot' was willing to accept a ruler who would ravish the womanhood of Scotland, embezzle the fortunes of the country, coerce the thanes. The volte-face on the part of Malcolm is astonishing.

> MALCOLM: I . . .
>
> . . . here abjure
> The taints and blames I laid upon myself
> For strangers to my nature.
>
> . . . . .
>
> . . . Myfirst flase speaking
> Was this upon myself.
>
> (Act IV, Scene iii)

It's all right, Macduff, you've passed the test. I was only joking. There's ten thousand English soldiers round the corner. No wonder Macduff says, 'Such welcome and unwelcome things at once, / 'Tis hard to reconcile.' Do we believe that Malcolm is telling the truth? That he has never before lied? It is immaterial. If he can lie like this to

Macduff, what sort of lies will he tell in the future to get his way?

Yet what sort of Scotland would Macduff have? He would have been willing to put up with the most extreme excesses of Malcolm's behaviour merely to have Macbeth out of the way. Women would have been raped, defiled — 'we have willing dames enough', says Macduff. But I would take your lands, rob your coffers, insists Malcolm.

> MACDUFF: . . . All these are portable,
> With other graces weighed.
> MALCOLM: But I have none.
> The king-becoming graces,
> As justice, verity, temperance, stableness,
> Bounty, perseverance, mercy, lowliness,
> Devotion, patience, courage, fortitude . . .
>
> (Act IV, Scene iii)

It takes a hell of a lot to put Macduff off. I wouldn't want to live in a country that was willing to accept the conditions that Malcolm imposes. No equality there. The contrast with Macbeth's view could not be more marked:

> . . . Then fly, false thanes
> And mingle with the English epicures.
>
> (Act V, Scene iii)

Macbeth indicates a pride in his own Scottishness and a total rejection of the fat, overfed English marching over the borders to usurp and dominate his homeland. The puritan versus the licentious. Duncan and Macbeth probably had more in common than meets the eye. Both believed in the innate sovereignty of Scotland, and Duncan would have been shocked to discover that his son had squandered his heritage. After all it is Macbeth at the start of the play who has saved Duncan's kingdom from being overrun by foreigners.

At the beginning of the play Duncan faces threats all round. Sensing a weakness in Duncan's rule, two thanes have stepped forward to claim the throne. Much has been made of Duncan's 'goodness', his 'saintliness', his 'chivalry'. The Duncan of history was a lot more ruthless, and reading between Shakespeare's lines there is more to Duncan than meets the eye. What is it about Duncan's reign that is so wonderful if two of his thanes are in rebellion and are in alliance with the invading Norwegian army under the command of the Norwegian king, Sweno, while the Western Isles, the Kerns and the Galloways are all up in arms against him? One is tempted to ask what is so rotten in the state of Scotland that he's got so many disparate factions threatening his rule. Or is it that it is merely a case of the old lion being tired? In Duncan's desperate defence of the realm there are echoes of other Shakespearean regimes – Old Hamlet's, Prospero's – whose dominions have fallen on hard times through neglect and are thus prey to invading and usurping forces. These foreign and domestic aggressors in *Macbeth* show that, no matter how saintly Duncan may be, he is just like other rulers who cling to power. That the defence of 'the gentle weal' is carried out by the barbaric arts of war and that these barbaric arts find their apotheosis in the man who is the most savage butcher of them all. Thank you cousin. 'Only I have left to say, / More is thy due than more than all can pay' (Act I, Scene iv).

In the whole Shakespearean canon, there is an obsession with what it is that motivates people to take power. The killing of the king is a primal urge in society, whether at a national or boardroom level. Shakespeare was fascinated by the gulf that exists between the thought of action and the act itself, and if, with Richard III, he reaches new heights of butchery, then *Macbeth* begins where Richard leaves off. Notwithstanding Macbeth's conscience, his need to murder Duncan is imperative. And, if Hamlet attempts to objectify, to analyse, then Macbeth is 'In blood stepp'd in so far', that there is only one inevitable path to the end. He is the most extreme of Shakespeare's creations. There is no death speech, no soliloquy, no recantation, only a belief that, as a man, he had to act as he did. He goes heroically, existentially, to his death, flying in the face of what he knows is about to happen, symbolically replacing the Cawdor of the beginning of the play, as he had replaced him in title, of whom it was said, 'Nothing in his life / Became him like the leaving it'.

Could not such energy and poetic drive have been used otherwise? In Macbeth's demonic descent into the hell of civil butchery, and in his desperate search to give coherence to the blackness that wells up in his soul, we find echoes of Schiller's Franz Moor in *Die Raüber* who says 'God forgive me, I am no ordinary murderer.'

Like father like son. Duncan gets Macbeth to do his dirty work, Malcolm uses Macduff. Macbeth, though, is paying a 'soldier's debt'. And what a warrior.

> . . . But all's too weak:
> For brave Macbeth – well he deserves that name –
> Disdaining fortune, with his brandished steel,
> Which smoked with bloody execution,
> Like valour's minion carved out his passage
> Till he faced the slave –
> Which ne'er shook hands, nor bade farewell to him
> Till he unseamed him from the nave to the chops,
> And fixed his head upon our battlements.
>
> (Act I, scene ii)

A positive orgy of savagery. And later in the same scene the sergeant says:

> So they
> Doubly redoubled strokes upon the foe.
> Except they meant to bathe in reeking wounds
> Or memorize another Golgotha
> I cannot tell.
> – But I am faint; my gashes cry for help.

Such is the importance of the news that no one has been the least concerned that the poor chap is almost bleeding to death. Duncan says, only now concerned for his welfare:

> So well thy words become thee as thy wounds,
> They smack of honour both. Go get him surgeons.

'Bellona's bridegroom', Macbeth has saved Duncan's bacon. His tottering regime has been rescued by the barbaric heroism of one man – well, plus Banquo. Well may Duncan call him '. . . valient cousin! Worthy Gentleman!' For the 'gentle weal' is dependent on a worthy gentleman who was ready

> . . .to bathe in reeking wounds
> Or memorize another Golgotha.

He honours all his noblemen; he honours in particular his most powerful subject at the moment of his greatest triumph. And yet, in that moment of Macbeth's triumph, Duncan does an extraordinary thing. At the point where Macbeth might reasonably expect to be named the successor to the throne of Scotland (there being no automatic succession, the kingship passing by vote or designation), Duncan produces an astute political rabbit out of his hat:

> . . . Sons, kinsmen, thanes,
> And you whose places are the nearest, know
> We will establish our estate upon
> Our eldest, Malcolm . . .

> (Act I, Scene iv)

What a hammer blow this is to Macbeth we learn from his soliloquy after the event.

> . . . That is a step
> On which I must fall down, or else o'erleap,
> For in my way it lies.

> (Act I, Scene iv)

He might reasonably have expected the succession to fall to him, and so might his companions and thanes. For, prior to this, we have no evidence of anything other than that Macbeth was very popular, a trifle unimaginative perhaps, but much liked, and that his one great attribute was that of being a magnificent warrior, the saviour of the kingdom. Duncan, having survived the traitorous attack on behalf of two of his thanes, decides that maybe the time is coming when he will lose his kingship and hastens to cement it by naming his son. Even in triumph Duncan feels himself to be vulnerable and psychologically moves to protect himself. This 'naming' is important because it implies a legitimacy of inheritance that is in not in fact there, the successor being arbitrarily chosen by the king in power. This of course often meant handing down to the next of kin, but if the king died without 'naming', then the thanes elected the successor. (Compare Hamlet's position *vis-á-vis* the throne of Denmark.) It is this 'naming' of Malcolm that undoes Duncan. There is a devastating irony when Duncan, on receipt of the news of Cawdor's treachery, looks into the face of Malcolm his son and says:

> There's no art
> To find the mind's construction in the face:
> He was a gentleman on whom I built
> An absolute trust.

(Act I Scene iv)

He is looking into the face of the man who turns out to be the most consummate liar of them all.

* * *

What of the prophecies of 'the weird sisters'? Notwithstanding Lady Macbeth's belief that the events of the play are the result of 'Fate and metaphysical aid', what we actually see is a series of man-made choices, decisions taken without a fate or a fury in sight. The witches appear at just the right psychological moment, at the point where Macbeth and Banquo are riding across the heath, high on killing, exhilarated after the bloodbath of the battle. The seeds of his downfall and his ambition are already contained within Macbeth himself: the savagery, the power released by the strength in his arm. The blood lust, the ambition, the belief in invincibility. That seed is nurtured by the weird sisters, but it would not have grown to fruition if the thought had not already been present in Macbeth. His is an existential choice: he chooses to make the witches' prophecy come true. He could have chosen to ignore their advice (after all, he doesn't *have* to kill Duncan), but they feed his ego, they feed his ambition. It is not so much a question of prophecy, more one of autosuggestion. The witches only articulate things that are known, or could be deduced. We the audience know before the witches tell Macbeth that he has been made Thane of Cawdor. It is common knowledge. And if Macbeth had been patient, despite Malcolm, the step over which he must stumble, it is odds-on that given his popularity and prowess, one day he would have possessed the 'golden round' legitimately. A bit old maybe. The witches only articulate the 'black and deep desires' that are already fermenting in his mind. Making the prophecies come to pass depends entirely on Macbeth's desire to make them concrete. The wish is father to the thought, though it may take a little while for him to put two and two together. (With a little help from his wife.)

> . . . equivocation of the fiend
> That lies like truth.

> (Act V, Scene v)

The supernatural element gradually weakens as the strength of Macbeth grows. The imaginary dagger, Banquo's ghost and the apparitions all gradually disappear, and witchery is replaced by the plausible and the practical. Ultimately, the two great prophecies, Birnam Wood coming to Dunsinane, and Macbeth succumbing to 'a man of no woman born' are confidence tricks. The first is no more than a tactical military exercise in camouflage that was well known in the history of European battles. If the story had not come such a long way in its power, it would be laughable. In the second, Macbeth meets his nemesis, not at the hands of a superman, someone 'not of woman born', but an ordinary mortal in the shape of Macduff born by Caesarean, 'who was from his mother's womb untimely ripped'. In such a closed and small community of ruling thanes the circumstances of Macduff's birth would have been universally known. Had Macbeth not at this moment been subject to his own psychological doubts and fears, and had he logically and pragmatically analysed the 'prophecies', he might have come to the right conclusions. The imagination for Shakespeare is a dark, primordial labyrinth where the battleground of our fantasies wrestles with the daylight of action. ('In the night, imagining some fear, / How easy is a bush supposed a bear!', *A Midsummer Night's Dream,* Act V, Scene i.) There are no miracles. Woods do not move. Men are born of women. Dragons are a myth. But, by then, his mind is too far gone, he has succumbed and become a victim, like Brutus, like Richard III, of his own fantasies and persuasions.

The witches, those 'black and midnight hags', complicate our reading of the story, imposing as they do a false trail of reliance on external forces to explain Macbeth's actions. Yet they themselves have their origin in entirely explicable circumstances, creatures on the fringes of society, outcasts. In Elizabethan terms, witches were often single women, spinsters, living on the outskirts of villages, midwives, nursemaids. Their magic is not black or satanic. It is practical, the use of herbs for healing. Some of the viler-sounding ingredients of the cauldron turn out to be nothing more than harmless country names for wild flowers and roots. But the witches represent a typical Shakespearean sociologic reversal of the natural order. Those with nothing ostensibly control the life of him who has everything. A contrast between those who have and those who have not. The single female was often thought to have supernatural powers which gave rise to the fear in men that she could be credited with certain kinds of knowledge to do with life and death. A society that does not give women power fears their mystery. In this kind of climate witchcraft grew as men came to fear this unknown power. James VI and I, who wrote a book on witchcraft, managed to have more witches killed during his reign than at any other time throughout British history.

As Terry Eagleton says:

> The witches are exiles from a society based on routine oppression and incessant warfare. They are poets, prophetesses and devotees of female cult. Radical separatists who scorn male power, they strike at the stable social, sexual and linguistic forms which the society of the play needs to survive. As their teasing riddles and deadly nonsense rhymes make plain, they scorn male power and lay bare the hollow sound and fury at its heart. Their words and bodies mock rigorous boundaries and make sport of fixed positions, unhinging received meanings as they dance, dissolve and rematerialise. Their rhyming jingles, their tantalising prophecies and the spectral dynasty of future kings they summon to torment his eyes, hold up an ironic mirror to the specifically male fantasies of supremacy and violence fostered in 'Bellona's bridegroom', by the cut-throat warrior's world which defines him. The witches cordon off and qualify Macbeth's thoughts and actions as symptomatic of the kind of life he had learned to lead, thwarting any urge we may feel to accept them without questioning their character or their causes.
>
> (*William Shakespeare*, 1986)

Lady Macbeth invokes the black art of witchcraft:

> Come, you spirits
> That tend on mortal thoughts, unsex me here.
>
> (Act I, Scene v)

Maleness is macho, women are weak. Lady Macbeth fears that her husband is not in fact the stuff of which ruthless individualists are made because he is 'too full o'the milk of human-kindness / To catch the nearest way.'

Here is a challenge to his masculinity, a gauntlet thrown down by his lady in the true spirit of a jousting knight, the Dark Age equivalent of the white feather. Macbeth, from being a hitherto unexceptional, uncreative person save for his physical prowess, unleashes a wild creative and poetic imagination by the one peacetime act of a single murder. Lady Macbeth has looked no further than the simple act of killing Duncan. Beyond that she has not seen what the consequences of killing a king might be.

Macbeth – 'To know my deed t'were best not know myself' – has looked into the future and seen that this one act of regicide will unleash a whole chain of killing. And what does Lady Macbeth think she is going to do? Sit on the throne in comfort for the rest of her days? As Macbeth came by the throne, so he might lose it. While Banquo lives – the only other figure privy to the prophecies, ambitious for himself, his son, waiting frustrated in the wings, being fobbed off continuously by the promise of a talk about things some day – there is danger.

Macbeth has already transgressed the bounds of moral acceptability once in time of peace. Killing in war is legitimate, of course. He has, through the strength of his fighting ability, killed and butchered, 'and seamed from the nave to the chops' a thousand opponents. What a good chap, they all cry. But this one act of killing in peacetime is unacceptable. Where is the moral line to be drawn? Kill a thousand in the name of some dubious cause and be praised? Or one, and be judged. 'God forgive me, I am no ordinary murderer.' The line, like the story of Macbeth, is as direct as an arrow – from Nietzsche, down through Schopenhauer, to Hitler et al. It is a question that we still must answer in the twenty-first century. Do we paradoxically admire the poetic imagination of Macbeth while celebrating his departure? Does he appeal to those latent forces that lie dormant within us all waiting to be unleashed? Duncan, Malcolm, Macbeth, Macduff - who would you choose? Hands up.

Though set in 1100 Shakespeare's play is rooted firmly in the politics of 1606. As Prince John in *Henry IV* Part Two signifies the passing of the heroic age of Hotspur, so the death of Macbeth prefigures the rise of Malcolm. No longer the 'boy' of Macbeth's contemptuous dismissal, he lays to rest the ghost of his father with a Bush-like 'peace and all that we long for'. The consequences are still being felt four hundred years later.

King Lear

the world turned upside down

I have never directed *King Lear*. I am not sure why, there have been several opportunities. The nearest I have come is a workshop in the woods in Taos in New Mexico with students from the Southern Methodist University, Dallas. (Lear staggering waist high in water along a stream bearing the body of Cordelia. Howl.)

There is something in the play that worries me. Each time I see it or read it I am conscious of the weight of opinion (only in the last fifty years, I have to add) that regards the play as Shakespeare's greatest achievement, his crowning masterpiece accomplished at the height of his powers in his great creative purple patch. I look at the fairy-tale structure – more than a passing resemblance to Cinderella minus the happy ending, try to get behind the less than soaring poetry, apply all the usual rules of political engagement that pertain to Shakespeare's power plays, recognise the kinship with Beckett, as a madman, a fool and a blind man wander the heath in a storm in a codified world comprised of *non sequitur* and subtext, and still I am uneasy. Why? For the engaged director, *Lear* seems to be the ultimate play about equality, examining as it does the way in which autocratic power ruthlessly divides and brings about the downfall of humanity.

There are in fact three versions of the play. There is the Quarto version published in 1608, known as Q1, or the 'Pide Bull Quarto'. And then there is the first Folio version published in 1623. The Folio contains a hundred lines not in the Quarto and the Quarto contains some three hundred lines not in the Folio. Both contain passages and lines that we would be very sorry to lose. Most editions combine the two texts thus constituting the third version of the play. Would the real *King Lear* please stand up?

For over three hundred years, until the second half of the twentieth century, the play was not regarded in any way as a masterpiece. It was imperfect and unplayable in the view of many. What is it in our own twenty-first-century culture that has reversed a view held over the years by poets, dramatists, critics, actors, theatregoers, Tolstoy and Dr Johnson alike? They can't all be blind and stupid. And was it Shakespeare himself who cut from both the Quarto and Folio versions some of the most famous lines?

If there is one play, then, that exemplifies more than any other the changing nature of historical perspective then it is *King Lear*. What do we mean by *King Lear* today? What did the seventeenth century mean? And which version are we talking about? I suspect that the thinking of the last fifty years that has catapulted *Lear* to the top of the critical tree has much to do with the globalised spread of war and the increasing awareness of what that means. The holocaust of 1939–45 and the involvement of the world in a struggle against the forces of Nazism, and now, the nightly beaming of battle and devastation into our living rooms under the auspices of the BBC and CNN, have brought a new universal awareness of the nihilistic mayhem in *King Lear*. Not that other eras were unaware of this, but today its images seem more present, more urgent. The more we recognise inhumanity and injustice, the more we witness the disintegration of the family unit, the more urgent and accessible the themes of *Lear* become, not because they were not understood in the past, but because they are now more to the fore and the imperfections of the play have become less important.

Shakespeare's play goes back to a time of pre-literature, to legend, of the tribal, Celtic world of hierarchy and division. It can be no coincidence that the date of the Quarto is given as 1608, the same year that James VI and I passed the Act of Union, bringing together all the warring factions of Great Britain and uniting them for the first time under one banner. Henceforth England, Scotland and

Wales would have to bury their religious, cultural and linguistic hatchets and lump it under Westminster. (It is significant that James's three children were the Duke of Albany, the Duke of Cornwall and Princess Elizabeth.) Four hundred years later the discontent that this caused reverberates in the Celtic lands today.

The story is simple enough, taken from an account of Geoffrey of Monmouth around the twelfth century. The old (pagan) king decides to divide up his kingdom, in this case Britain, between his three daughters, on the basis of how much love they are willing to accord him. He calls it his 'darker purpose'. Two come across, in his eyes, with the goods, one backs off. The kingdom is divided into two. The dissenter (now penniless) is taken up by the King of France and comes back with an army to try and claim the lot. The two ugly sisters bite the hand that feeds them and have their autocratic, tyrannical father thrown out of house and home to wander the heath in a storm, gradually going mad. He is joined by a fool, a blind man and another outcast posing as a beggar. Just about all of them end up dead. It was a bad move or what? And the moral is: If you are going to give your stuff away make sure you leave something for yourself. There is no good deed that goes unpunished, and there is none so ungrateful as those who have been unduly favoured. Make sure, out of self-interest, that you share equally. But that wasn't in Lear's nature, hence the tragedy.

Why does he give up the kingdom at this point? The theme is worked out with equal vituperation in *Timon of Athens*. Timon gives away his possessions to all and sundry and then, when he is broke, throws himself on the mercy of his erstwhile friends. Of course, the rats desert the ship. Love in Shakespeare is valued by land, possessions, gold, silver – anything but pure unalloyed emotion (well, rarely). So Lear comes to recognise Cordelia's love when it is too late.

But what was Cordelia doing returning with the French army to invade?

> **KENT: But true it is, from France there comes a power**
> **Into this scattered kingdom, who already,**
> **Wise in our negligence, have secret feet**

**In some of our best ports and are at point
To show their open banner.**

(Act III, Scene i)

What did Cordelia intend? Defeat the armies of Albany and Cornwall (Regan and Goneril) and return the kingdom to her father (who had given it away in the first place), or keep it for France? What would she have done with Regan and Goneril? Where would Lear have fitted in? For all she knows, at the point where we hear of the army, Lear is having a good time with his hundred knights rampaging up and down the land – authority without responsibility.

The play deals in inheritance through legitimacy. Once again the question is raised as to who are real and who are assumed parents. The offspring resulting from union with a wife are 'legitimate', those from union with a woman from outside marriage 'illegitimate', even though Edmund's conception was the occasion of 'great sport'. (Was his wife as good in bed? The implication is not.) However the mother–child relationship in the play is non-existent. The only source of love and authority is the father. Leaving aside Shakespeare's convenient pragmatic solution to the lack of females in his acting company, the conclusion must be that the best mother is an absent or dead mother. Goneril and Regan have no children. How old are they? Cordelia, the youngest, is the favourite – an afterthought? Are there fifteen to twenty years between her and her sisters? It gives a spur to the jealousy if there are.

Love is confused with lust. Edmund, a whore's son, born out of wedlock and 'sport', is belittled and passed over. Edgar is favoured. Britain is a paradise lost as Satan in the guise of Edmund becomes the most attractive character on offer, seducing male and female alike.

* * *

The play begins by reducing a land and its people to a map:

> **LEAR: Meantime, we shall express our darker purpose.**
> **Give me the map there. Know that we have divided**
> **In three our kingdom; and 'tis our fast intent**
> **To shake all cares and business from our age,**
> **Conferring them on younger strengths, while we**
> **Unburdened crawl toward death.**
>
> (Act I, Scene i)

The culture and terrain of this world are a few lines drawn on a piece of paper, an inhuman act to the level of the absurd as people and boundaries are shifted around at will and whim. Maps simplify, relegate culture to a few place-names. Here kingship is reduced to the level of a landlord, converting an old family home into three apartments. The theme is repeated in *Henry IV Part One*, where Hotspur, Glendower and Mortimer attempt to divide up the kingdom between them. The unreal world of the map is reduced to the level of farce, as Hotspur simply seeks to alter the course of the 'smug and silver Trent/. . . It shall not wind with such a deep indent because it 'cuts me from the best of all my land/A huge half-moon, a monstrous cantle out.' He'll have the river straightened. Easy. Just get the rubber and the pencil out. Change the world at a stroke. (In Geoffrey of Monmouth's account, Albany and Cornwall, the names of the dukes married to Regan and Goneril, are the old names for Scotland, and Wales and the West of England. Cordelia, in the play, presumably represents the rest of Britain.)

Lear's offer of land for love reduces emotion to a formula. Tell me in so many words how much you love me. Tap it in and the amount will measure on the screen.

> **GONERIL: Sir, I love you more than word can wield the matter,**
> **Dearer than eyesight, space, and liberty,**
> **Beyond what can be valued rich or rare,**
> **No less than life, with grace, health, beauty, honour,**

As much child e'er loved or father found;
A love that makes breath poor and speech unable;
Beyond all manner of 'so much' I love you.

(Act I, Scene i)

This is a mercenary world of calculation where words have a numeberic value. Add them all up at the end and see who has the highest score. Where emotion plays no part in the calculation, someone is always bound to come out a loser.

LEAR: . . . When she was dear to us we did hold her so;
But now her price is fallen.

(Act I, Scene i)

Love for land is a symptom of the material problems of the decaying system of kingship, into which Cordelia is unwilling to buy. It measures price at the expense of value; Britain is a cake to be cut into three with Lear retaining the right still to eat it.

LEAR: Ourself by monthly course,
With reservation of an hundred knights,
By you to be sustained, shall our abode
Make with you by due turn.

(Act I, Scene i)

Having it all ways or what? The metaphor of land for love and price for value continues over the vexed question of Lear's hundred knights. The daughter who allows him the largest number is the one who loves him best. Sorry dad. Fifty is the limit.

LEAR: I prithee, daughter, do not make me mad.
I will not trouble thee, my child. Farewell.
We'll no more meet, no more see one another.
But yet thou art my flesh, my blood, my daughter –
Or rather a disease that's in my flesh,

Which I must needs call mine. Thou art a boil,
A plague-sore, or embossèd carbuncle,
In my corrupted blood. But I'll not chide thee.
Let shame come when it will, I do not call it.
I do not bid the thunder-bearer shoot,
Nor tell tales of thee to high-judging Jove.
Mend when thou canst, be better at thy leisure;
I can be patient, I can stay with Regan,
I and my hundred knights.

(Act II, Scene iv)

In a reverse auction his emotions are auctioned off and knocked down to the one that allows him the least number. One hundred — one hundred — any decrease on a hundred? Fifty, do I hear fifty? Twenty-five on the right. Twenty-five — NONE! Sold to the lady in the iron petticoat. Terms and conditions apply. Big Brother has voted you out. You must leave the house instantly.

CORNWALL: Let us withdraw; 'twill be a storm.
REGAN: This house is little; the old man and's people
Cannot be well bestowed.

(Act II, Scene iv)

People here are so many cattle. There is no King like an ex-King.

But ethics cannot be reduced to mere numbers. This is a male world that cedes power to the women, where stability depends on legitimacy, and both Lear and Gloucester become involved in the struggle to secure succession. Illegitimate Edmund seethes with emotion and far from suffering the yoke around his neck fights back in a bitter machiavellian counter-move to secure his inheritance.

EDMUND: Thou, Nature, art my goddess; to thy law
My services are bound. . . .
. . . . .
Legitimate Edgar, I must have your land.
Our father's love is to the bastard Edmund

123

As to the legitimate. Fine word 'legitimate'!
Well my 'legitimate', if this letter speed
And my intention thrive, Edmund the base
Shall top the legitimate. I grow. I prosper.
Now gods stand up for bastards!

(Act I, Scene ii)

* * *

This is an old Shakespearean trick — Richard III, Shylock, Iago, Macbeth — a long line of characters from the dark side of the moon who act from motives of exclusion. Orthodox, conservative society has excluded these outsiders and they fight back the only way they know how, by punishing the perpetrators. The message is that a community and a system must embrace differences, have moral and cultural equality and harmony, or it will shore up problems for itself. The boil will burst if it is not treated.

Edmund stands for nature on the rampage. If he is not accommodated then he will be trouble. Gloucester, yet another 'good old man', belittles him in his presence, is patronising and disparaging:

GLOUCESTER: His breeding, sir, hath been at my charge. I have so often blushed to acknowledge him that now I am brazed to it.
KENT: I cannot conceive you.
GLOUCESTER: Sir, this young fellow's mother could; whereupon she grew round-wombed, and had indeed, sir, a son for her cradle ere she had a husband for her bed. Do you smell a fault?
KENT: I cannot wish the fault undone, the issue of it being so proper.
GLOUCESTER: But I have a son, sir, by order of law, some year elder than this, who yet is no dearer in my account. Though this knave came something saucily to the world,

before he was sent for, yet was his mother fair; there was good sport at his making, and the whoreson must be acknowledged.

(Act I, Scene i)

If this is how Gloucester treats him on this occasion, can we wonder at the cumulative effect of this constant derision? 'Speak what we feel, not what we ought to say', says Edgar at the close. 'We that are young / Shall never see so much nor live so long.' He returns us to the beginning where Goneril and Regan utter what they think they should say, while Cordelia says 'nothing', speaks what she feels. If I should marry, she says, whom should I love, my father or my husband? My sisters are fools:

CORDELIA: You have begot me, bred me, loved me.
I return those duties back as are right fit,
Obey you, love you, and most honour you.
Why have my sisters husbands, if they say
They love you all? Haply, when I shall wed,
That lord whose hand must take my plight shall carry
Half my love with him, half my care and duty.
Sure I shall never marry like my sisters,
To love my father all.

(Act I, Scene i)

In this Cordelia shows great prescience, for neither Goneril nor Regan loves her husband enough to stay faithful to him, the glamour of Edmund proving too much for them as they implode with jealousy. In true fairy-story style, the moral should be that good will out, if it weren't for the fact that, Edgar excluded, all those with a shred of goodness in them end up dead or maimed. This is wholly compatible with Shakespeare's bleak view of the world and *Realpolitik*. Cordelia is no Fortinbras, Alcibides or Richmond. No, France has gone home leaving Cordelia alone. There is too much danger in turning your back on government and going abroad at a crucial time even if it is to fight your wife's battles and Britain is the prize, as Richard II found out to his cost.

* * *

Cordelia will not play the word game. 'Nothing', she says.

> LEAR: Nothing?
> CORDELIA: Nothing.
> LEAR: Nothing will come of nothing. Speak again.
> CORDELIA: Unhappy that I am, I cannot heave
> My heart into my mouth. I love your majesty
> According to my bond, no more nor less.

> (Act I, Scene i)

Language versus silence. Education has narrowed the gap between emotion and intellect. We now have a shorthand for everything and communication is often reduced to words of a few syllables. What colour is it? Red. We have an instant image of a sort of homogeneous catch-all generalised red — no texture, no character to it. How does it feel, taste, smell, look? What are its dimensions? Red. Reduced. Nothing. Lear learns to express his emotions through the use of language and only at the cost of his reason.

> LEAR: . . . You think I'll weep.
> No, I'll not weep.
> I have full cause of weeping; but this heart
> Shall break into a hundred thousand flaws
> Or ere I'll weep. O Fool, I shall go mad!

> (Act II, Scene iv)

When at last he is stripped of everything, wandering the heath homeless in the storm, 'a bare forked animal', then and only then does he appreciate the value of sharing.

> LEAR: Poor naked wretches, whereso'er you are,
> That bide the pelting of this pitiless storm,
> How shall your houseless heads and unfed sides,
> Your looped and windowed raggedness, defend you
> From seasons such as these? O, I have ta'en

Too little care of this! Take physic, pomp;
Expose thyself to feel what wretches feel,
That thou mayst shake the superflux to them
And show the heavens more just.

(Act III, Scene iv)

The heath and the mind shelter the homeless on an equal footing and as he staggers brokenly from prison bearing the dead body of Cordelia in his arms, then and only then does he realise the inadequacy of language to express the well of emotion and love that he feels:

LEAR: Howl, howl, howl! O, you are men of stones!
Had I your tongues and eyes I'd use them so
That heaven's vault should crack. She's gone for ever.
I know when one is dead and when one lives;
She's dead as earth. Lend me a looking-glass;
If that her breath will mist or stain the stone,
Why then she lives.

(Act V, Scene iii)

Nothing. In death Cordelia's silence says everything.

* * *

Having said 'nothing', Cordelia disappears from the play until almost the end and her place and voice are effectively occupied by the Fool.

FOOL: Sirrah, I'll teach thee a speech.
LEAR: Do.
FOOL: Mark it, nuncle:
Have more than thou showest,
Speak less that thou knowest,
Lend less than thou owest,

Ride more than thou goest,
Learn more than thou trowest,
Set less than thou throwest;
Leave thy drink and thy whore
And keep in-a-door,
And thou shalt have more
Than two tens to a score.

KENT: This is nothing, Fool.

FOOL: Then 'tis like the breath of an unfee'd lawyer: you gave me nothing for't. Can you make no use of nothing, nuncle?

LEAR: Why no, boy. Nothing can be made out of nothing.

FOOL: [to Kent] Prithee tell him; so much the rent of his land comes to. He will not believe a Fool.

LEAR: A bitter fool!

FOOL: Dost thou know the difference, my boy, between a bitter fool and a sweet one?

LEAR: No, lad; teach me.

FOOL: That lord that counselled thee
To give away thy land,
Come place him here by me;
Do thou for him stand.
The sweet and bitter fool
Will presently appear:
The one in motley here,
The other found out – there.

LEAR: Dost thou call me a fool, boy?

FOOL: All thy other titles thou hast given away; that thou wast born with.

(Act I, Scene iv)

His is the lone voice raised in Lear's company that articulates Lear's foolishness. The Fool, non-rational, is wise.

FOOL: . . . Nuncle, give me an egg, and I'll give thee two crowns.

LEAR: What two crowns shall they be?

FOOL: Why, after I have cut the egg i'th'middle and eat up

the meat, the two crowns of the egg. When thou clovest thy crown i'th'middle, and gavest away both parts, thou borest thine ass on thy back o'er the dirt. Thou hadst little wit in thy bald crown when thou gavest thy golden one away.

(Act I, Scene iv)

'He will not believe a fool.' Like Feste in *Twelfth Night* and Touchstone in *As You Like It*, the Fool acts as a counterbalance to the action, keeping us up to speed on the issues at stake. This is nowhere more apparent than at the end of Act III, Scene ii, when the Fool addresses the audience directly:

FOOL: . . . I'll speak a prophecy ere I go:
When priests are more in word than matter,
When brewers mar their malt with water,
When nobles are their tailors' tutors,
No heretics burned, but wenches' suitors –
Then shall the realm of Albion
Come to great confusion.
When every case in law is right,
No squire in debt, nor no poor knight,
When slanders do not live in tongues,
Nor cutpurses come not to throngs,
When usurers tell their gold i'the field,
And bawds and whores do churches build –
Then comes the time, who lives to see't,
That going shall be used with feet.
This prophecy Merlin shall make; for I live before his time.

(Act III, Scene ii)

The world turned upside down. There is a bitter cataclysmic quality to this speech of two halves, which on the one hand posits a world of peace and harmony, and on the other one that consists of nihilistic devastation. As the world of the stage is divided between the play and the audience, so the Fool captures the sense of both illusion and reality, examining once again the power of the imagination and the actuality. This contradiction seems to me to be the nub and crux at the heart of *King Lear*, turning the very idea of a class-divided society on its head, a golden thread that runs through all the plays.

> **GLOUCESTER: I see it feelingly.**
> **LEAR: What, art mad? A man may see how this world goes**
> **with no eyes. Look with thine ears. See how yon justice rails**
> **upon yon simple thief. Hark in thine ear – change places**
> **and, handy-dandy, which is the justice, which is the thief?**
> **Thou hast seen a farmer's dog bark at a beggar?**
> **GLOUCESTER: Ay, sir.**
> **LEAR: And the creature run from the cur? There thou**
> **mightst behold the great image of authority: a dog's obeyed**
> **in office.**
> **Thou rascal beadle, hold thy bloody hand.**
> **Why dost thou lash that whore? Strip thy own back.**
> **Thou hotly lusts to use her in that kind**
> **For which thou whipp'st her. The usurer hangs the cozener.**
> **Thorough tattered clothes great vices do appear;**
> **Robes and furred gowns hide all. Plate sins with gold,**
> **And the strong lance of justice hurtless breaks;**
> **Arm it in rags, a pygmy's straw does pierce it.**
>
> **(Act IV, Scene v)**

Although the story seems to conform to the conservative restoration of order through the triumph of 'legitimate Edgar' over 'the bastard Edmund' who despises 'the plague of custom', the text ultimately rejects a view of a world that is such, in favour of one that is built on equality and partnership rather than exploitation and dislocation.

It is too simplistic to follow Orwell's unimaginative interpretation based on the theory of the fatal flaw, which determines a view of the play that merely makes the cataclysmic consequences Lear's fault for the stupendous folly of surrendering his sovereignty in the first place. This wagging finger, 'I told you so' approach that categorises much of orthodox thinking on Shakespeare's protagonists makes you wonder why he wrote the plays in the first place, if it is only to show that those who challenge established order get what they deserve. Such a reading of *Lear* misses the whole point of a play that puts an all-powerful patriarchal ruler through the mangle of traumatic experience, turning on its head the whole question of kingship and the unequal distribution of wealth and power associated with it. Lear comes to an understanding of what it means to have an egalitarian society: that a world governed by the dominant ideologies of war, economic and sexual exploitation is patently wrong. It looks forward to an era when human beings may act with understanding and compassion and not be caught up in the inevitability of the dog-eat-dog syndrome, one that allies itself with the mad, the blind, the poor, the homeless, the powerless, the disenfranchised, and with all those who 'with best meaning have incurred the worst'. If ever there were a play for today's leaders, it is *King Lear*. They would do well to read and see it, in order to understand the consequences of the needless suffering and pain they inflict by pursuing imperial and global economic goals. Maybe I shouldn't worry.

I am indebted to Terence Hawkes for some of the thinking in this essay. (Terence Hawkes, King Lear: Writers and their Work, Northcote House 1995).

The Taming
of the Shrew
a male wish-fulfilment dream of revenge

Probably no other play in the entire canon has aroused such divergent opinion and passion in the last twenty years as *The Taming of the Shrew*. For many it is a barbaric document dedicated to male domination and brutality, a perfect example of Shakespeare the conservative. However, those who believe it should be kept locked in its Elizabethan cupboard to be viewed only from an historical perspective, a treatise on the humiliation of women – keep 'em in their place, if they complain bash them – are themselves contributing to a species of conservatism that is the obverse side of the same coin. To shut up literature of any kind is the sharp end of censorship, and the burning or banning of books and the shutting out of debate are perilously close to a world to which they would be horrified to subscribe. A reading of the other plays, never mind the *Shrew* itself, makes it abundantly clear to the most hardened misogynist that Shakespeare carried not just a torch for women's rights but lit a bloody big bonfire.

The Taming of the Shrew cannot in the twenty-first century be looked on as a domestic, marital comedy, with an erring wife rightly and meekly subjecting herself to the will of her husband, wrapped up in comedy and fun as in the Burton and Taylor film. It has to be viewed as the ruthless subduing of a woman by a man in a violent excess of male savagery, couched in the form of a class wish-fulfilment dream of revenge.

In this, it is much the same as *The Tempest*, but the starting point is the other end of the social scale. In *The Tempest*, Prospero, the Duke, is thrown out of Milan for not ruling the state properly. In the *Shrew*, Christopher Sly, a drunken tinker, is thrown out of a pub for breaking glasses. The key to the play lies in the very first scene, the Induction, often cut (as in Greg Doran's 2003 Bridget Jones production for the RSC and the all female version at the Globe Theatre), but which is in fact crucial to our understanding of the class structure of the play.

A drunken tinker is thrown out of a pub by a woman (the lady of the house). In a society that is basically controlled by males, this is the first indignity suffered by a man who has nothing – a tinker, a pauper, who has no money, drunk every night, humiliated at the hands of a woman. He protests that he is of royal lineage, descended from a long line of Norman tinkers. The hostess says 'So you won't pay for the glasses?' 'No I won't.' 'Right, I'm going to call the police.' 'OK, go and call the police and see what happens.' And then he falls asleep. Now, contained in those few lines is the essential character-conflict of the play. Christopher Sly has an inferiority complex about his position – social, financial and to do with the reversal of what he sees as the rightful role of a man in a world where men are dominant. As he sleeps, out of the dark emerge some huntsmen:

LORD: Hunstman, I charge thee, tender well my hounds.
Breathe Merriman, the poor cur is embossed,
And couple Clowder with the deep-mouthed brach.
Saw'st thou not, boy, how Silver made it good
At the hedge corner, in the coldest fault?
I would not lose the dog for twenty pound.
FIRST HUNTSMAN: Why, Belman is as good as he, my lord.
He cried upon it at the merest loss,
And twice today picked out the dullest scent.
Trust me, I take him for the better dog.
LORD: Thou art a fool. If Echo were as fleet,

I would esteem him worth a dozen such.
But sup them well, and look unto them all.
Tomorrow I intend to hunt again.

(Induction 1)

The huntsmen are talking about their dogs, betting on them: 'I would not lose the dog for twenty pound', almost the exact same sentiment expressed in the final scene, where the men bet on the women. The link between this moment of dogs and wives is of paramount importance.

HORTENSIO: . . . What's the wager?
LUCENTIO: Twenty crowns.
PETRUCHIO: Twenty crowns?
I'll venture so much of my hawk or hound,
But twenty times so much upon my wife.
LUCENTIO: A hundred then.
HORTENSIO: Content.
PETRUCHIO: A match! 'Tis done.

(Act V, Scene ii)

Huntsmen hunt stags or hares, husbands hunt wives. And not only that, when the huntsman says, 'Tomorrow I intend to hunt again', there is a forewarning, a presaging of what is about to happen. The dog of today that will tear down its quarry, will, in the shape of Petruchio tomorrow, tear down Kate.

LORD: What's here? One dead, or drunk? See, doth he breathe?
SECOND HUNTSMAN: He breathes, my lord. Were he not warmed with ale,
This were a bed but cold to sleep so soundly.
LORD: O monstrous beast, how like a swine he lies!
Grim death, how foul and loathsome is thine image!
Sirs, I will practise on this drunken man.
What think you, if he were conveyed to bed,
Wrapped in sweet clothes, rings put upon his fingers,

A most delicious banquet by his bed,
And brave attendants near him when he wakes,
Would not the beggar then forget himself?
FIRST HUNTSMAN: Believe me, lord. I think he cannot choose.
SECOND HUNTSMAN: It would seem strange unto him when he waked.
LORD: Even as a flattering dream of worthless fancy.
Then take him up, and manage well the jest.
Carry him gently to my fairest chamber,
And hang it round with all my wanton pictures.
Balm his foul head with warm distillèd waters,
And burn sweet wood to make the lodging sweet.
Procure me music ready when he wakes,
To make a dulcet and a heavenly sound.
And if he chance to speak, be ready straight.
And with a low submissive reverence
Say 'What is it your honour will command?'
Let one attend him with a silver basin
Full of rose-water and bestrewed with flowers,
Another bear the ewer, the third a diaper,
And say 'Will't please your lordship cool your hands?'
Some one be ready with a costly suit,
And ask him what apparel he will wear.
Another tell him of his hounds and horse,
And that his lady mourns at his disease.
Persuade him that he hath been lunatic,
And when he says he is Sly, say that he dreams,
For he is nothing but a mighty lord.

(Induction 1)

The huntsmen come out of the dark and say, 'We will transport this man to an unknown world, a foreign paradise of gentility, of nobility, of privilege. We will invest in him all the accoutrements of a nobleman, of a lord.' At this point, the wish-fulfilment dream of Sly is already taking shape. As he sleeps and dreams he begins to project himself, in his fantasy, into a position of power, authority and affluence.

Gradually, at the hands of the huntsmen, he loses his lower-class complex and is transformed. The dawning, the awakening, the realisation that he is all those things that were once beyond his reach, brings about a change in manner, language and confidence.

SLY: Am I a lord and have I such a lady?
Or do I dream? Or have I dreamed till now?
I do not sleep. I see, I hear, I speak.
I smell sweet savours and I feel soft things.
Upon my life, I am a lord indeed,
And not a tinker nor Christophero Sly.
Well, bring our lady hither to our sight,
And once again, a pot o'th'smallest ale.
SECOND SERVINGMAN: Will't please your mightiness to wash your hands?
O, how we joy to see your wit restored!
O, that once more you know but what you are!
These fifteen years you have been in a dream,
Or when you waked, so waked as if you slept.
SLY: These fifteen years! By my fay, a goodly nap.
But did I never speak of all that time?
FIRST SERVINGMAN: O, yes, my lord, but very idle words,
For though you lay here in this goodly chamber,
Yet would you say ye were beaten out of door,
And rail upon the hostess of the house,
And say you would present her at the leet [court],
Because she brought stone jugs and no seal'd quarts.
Sometimes you would call out for Cicely Hacket.
SLY: Ay, the woman's maid of the house.
THIRD SERVINGMAN: Why, sir, you know no house, nor no such maid,
Nor no such men as you have reackoned up,
As Stephen Sly, and old John Naps of Greece,
And Peter Turph, and Henry Pimpernell,
And twenty more such names and men as these,
Which never were nor no man ever saw.
SLY: Now Lord be thankèd for my good amends.
ALL: Amen.

(Induction 2)

137

Dream. Sleep. Sleep. Dream. The world of *The Tempest* is never far away. Oh that we could live forever in our heads, but we have bad dreams. We are bounded in a nutshell.

A number of key lines. Fifteen years, the length of time that Sly himself could have been married. The obsession that he has with the woman of the house who has thrown him out of the pub: 'You would say you were beaten out of the door, and rail upon the hostess of the house, and say you would present her at the court.' A repetition of what he says immediately prior to falling asleep. In his dream, that same paranoid obsession consumes him, that desire for male revenge. 'Sometimes you'd call out for Cicely Hacket.' 'Aye, the woman's maid of the house, that's the one I'd like to get.' 'Why, you know no such house, nor no such maid.' They channel his paranoia.

A play is presented for Sly's benefit. And contained in that play, is the very mirror image of the situation that he, himself, has been replaying over and over again in his mind: the story of a man demonstrating how to tame a woman. This is what you do.

* * *

Now, let us examine a scene that isn't in *The Taming of the Shrew*; it comes from *The Taming of a Shrew*, a play which most commentators now accept is an early version by Shakespeare, which contains a number of scenes that were left out of the Folio edition when it was first produced in 1623. In the very last scene of the play, Petruchio has left with Kate, the players have disappeared, Sly is still asleep on the ground. The play is over. It is six o'clock in the morning with the dawn coming up. Sly, dew-decked on the dank ground, discovered by the Tapster, is waked from his drunken stupor.

TAPSTER: Now the dark of night is ever past and dawning day appears in the crystal sky, now must I haste abroad. Soft, what's this? What, Sly? Oh wondrous. He's lain here all night? I'll wake him. I think he's starved by this, but that his

138

belly was so stuff'd with ale. What ho, Sly! Wake, shame!

SLY: Sirra, give us some more wine. What? All the play is gone? Am I not a lord?

TAPSTER: A lord? With a moraine. Come on, thou drunken still.

SLY: Who's this? Tapster! Oh lord, sir, I've had the bravest dream tonight that ever thou heardest in all thy life.

TAPSTER: Aye, marry, but you'd best get you home, for your wife will thrash you for dreaming here tonight.

SLY: Will she? [*Laughs*] I know now how to tame a shrew. I dreamt upon it all this night till now, and thou must wake me out of the best dream that ever I had in my life! But I'll to my wife presently and tame her to, and if she anger me . . .

TAPSTER: Hey, tarry, Sly. I'm going with thee and know the rest of thy story.

Sly wakes up and says to the Tapster: 'I've had the best dream I've ever had in my life. I've dreamt how to tame a shrew', and the Tapster says, 'You'd better get home to your old woman, 'cos you won't half cop it.' He says, 'Oh-ho no, I know how to tame a shrew now, I'm going to show her what for.' And the Tapster says; 'Ho, ho I'm going to come with you, this I've got to see, baby.' Because he knows that as soon as Sly goes home and walks into that kitchen, he's going to bang on the table and say, 'Where's, my breakfast woman?' And his wife is going to say, 'What do you mean by coming home at this time of night and shouting for your breakfast – get out!'

Suddenly Sly is back where he started, the dream has come full circle. It has all been in his head; the Prospero of the pub. The waking moment, the diffusion of the fantasy, is different from the reality. Thought and action, the discrepancy between them, is one of the major themes of the plays. The wish-fulfilment dream of Christopher Sly is a direct link to Petruchio and the taming of Kate. Only with this difference; in his dream he can, in his life, he can't

* * *

Sly/Petruchio. As the play/dream unfolds let us examine his reasons for embarking on the taming venture. We have already been introduced to Kate and the premise of the shrew – her wildness and her unorthodox behaviour. That she behaves as she does is indisputable. What is interesting is the psychological reason for why she behaves as she does. It is no use, for example, to try and turn Shylock into a nice man in an attempt to avoid anti-Semitism. It is much more important to understand the political and social reasons that have turned him into the vengeful figure that he is. Pretty soon you uncover a devastating indictment of the appalling class-behavioural politics of that bunch of bastards on the Rialto.

We have also met, crucially, the person that Shakespeare calls 'The Prize'. This is how Bianca, the younger daughter of Baptista is termed on the title page: 'The Prize'. And Baptista cannot let 'The Prize', Bianca, be married until he has found a husband for Katherina. (Compare the Nurse's description of Juliet: 'He that can lay hold on her, will have the chinks.') Obviously, if Bianca is Baptista's bargaining power, then he cannot possibly run the risk of Katherina being on the shelf for the rest of her days. He must obtain the best for both his daughters, get as much money and land as possible. Keep the Baptista estates and wealth pile growing. This is the point at which Petruchio enters.

PETRUCHIO: Antonio, my father, is deceased.
And I have thrust myself into this maze,
Happily to wive and thrive as best I may.
Crowns in my purse I have, and goods at home,
And so am come abroad to see the world.
HORTENSIO: Petruchio, shall I then come roundly to thee
And wish thee to a shrewd ill-flavoured wife?
Thou'dst thank me but little for my counsel,
And yet I'll promise thee she shall be rich,
And very rich. But th'art too much my friend,
And I'll not wish thee to her.
PETRUCHIO: Signor Hortensio, 'twixt such friends as we
Few words suffice; and therefore, if thou know
One rich enough to be Petruchio's wife –

As wealth is burden of my wooing dance –
Be she as foul as was Florentius' love,
As old as Sybil, and as curst and shrewd
As Socrates' Xanthippe, or a worse,
She moves me not, or not removes at least
Affection's edge in me, were she as rough
As are the swelling Adriatic seas.
I come to wive it wealthily in Padua; I
If wealthily, then happily in Padua.
GRUMIO: Nay, look you, sir, he tells you flatly what his mind
is. Why, give him gold enough and marry him to a puppet or
an aglet-baby, or an old trot with ne'er a tooth in her head,
though she have as many diseases as two and fifty horses.
Why, nothing comes amiss, so money comes withal.

(Act I, Scene ii)

He's come to wive and thrive as best he may. If she's rich, then it doesn't matter what she looks like, whether foul, old, cursed, shrewd or worse. In other words, looks and behaviour are immaterial as long as she's got money. 'Nothing comes amiss, so money comes withal'. And Petruchio answers, 'Thou knowest not gold's effect.' Even before meeting Katherina he is hyped up, ready to take her on. Ready to possess her, her dowry, her wealth and her estates. A proper Elizabethan condition, I hear you cry. What's wrong with that? Shakespeare was only observing the social condition of his time. Petruchio marries her. So what? Rich families got richer and richer by bargaining and bartering their daughters to make sure they gained more power and influence.

But Shakespeare's treatment is radically different. As soon as Katherina is out of the way, Baptista bargains with young Tranio (disguised as Lucentio, his master) and with the octogenarian Gremio, as to who can give the most for his daughter's hand. 'Now I'll play a merchant's part.' Bianca will go to the highest bidder. Accepted practices in Elizabethan society are mirrored in this play, but are taken to a violent extreme in order to demonstrate the absurdity of the proposition. The ostensibly comic auction is a terrifying indictment of a system that will see a young girl married either to an eligible youth or a doddery old man, merely on the flip of a coin. *Romeo and Juliet* is based on the same premise: Juliet must be married to the wealthy nephew of the Prince and there is no question of her having any say in the matter whatsoever. This historical condition ignores the question of individual freedom of choice, and it is this freedom that Shakespeare explores from his egalitarian and humanist standpoint.

Petruchio marries Katherina. At the first sign of dissent, he lays down his submission laws:

> **PETRUCHIO: Nay, look not big, nor stamp nor stare, nor fret,**
> **I will be master of what is mine own.**
> **She is my goods, my chattels, she is my house,**
> **My household stuff, my field, my barn,**
> **My horse, my ox, my ass, my any thing,**
> **And here she stands. Touch her whoever dare.**
>
> **(Act III, Scene ii)**

That then is the definitive statement of possession – of owning lock, stock and barrel some *thing*, not some*body*, but some *thing*, using Katherina merely as a commodity as, later, Bianca is used by Baptista. Pretty nasty stuff. Ruthless, serious, and any comedy that arises comes from the commitment on the part of the actor to these beliefs of Petruchio, and not through a tongue-in-cheek attitude to the writing. In this way, not only are the women debased, but men too.

Petruchio has succeeded in his first objective – to get the ring on the finger and obtain the money, 'the Specialities', that were drawn up with Baptista before his first meeting with Kate, the business deal. He now embarks on the next part of his plan, which is to separate her from the society with which she is familiar and disorientate her through a form of processing, as in the Brian Forbes film *The Stepford Wives*, where the women are sent to a 'taming house'. Disorientation, classical anti-terrorist techniques of third-degree torture and brain-washing. And here is the question on which the answer depends, as to whether the *Shrew* is a modern play or not. Was Petruchio successful? If, as many arguments go, Kate got the man she deserved, the man she wanted, the only one who could match her guts, fiery spirit and self-willed determination, then the conclusion is dangerously close to the argument that women only get raped because they wish to be. That Kate is a willing participant in a masochistic experience.

Can the marriage be happy? Is it finally love? Or is it ultimately the brutalising and crushing of an independent spirit by a physical and mental force? The revenge of a male society on any woman who steps out of line? The class and sexual frustrations of Christopher Sly, tinker? Consider the impassioned speech by Emilia in *Othello* on the consequences of the inequality and injustice built into marriage:

> EMILIA: But I do think it is their husbands' faults
> If wives do fall. Say that they slack their duties,
> And pour our treasures into foreign laps;
> Or else break out in peevish jealousies,
> Throwing restraint upon us; or say they strike us,
> Or scant our former having in despite –
> Why, we have galls, and though we have some grace,
> Yet have we some revenge. Let husbands know
> Their wives have sense like them: they see and smell,
> And have their palates both for sweet and sour
> As husbands have. What is it that they do,
> When they change us for others? Is it sport?
> I think it is. And doth affection breed it?
> I think it doth. Is't frailty that thus errs?
> It is so too. And have not we affections,
> Desires for sport, and frailty, as men have?
> Then let them use us well: else let them know
> The ills we do, their ills instruct us so.
>
> (Act IV, Scene iii)

Who in the face of such a plea can deny Shakespeare his place in the annals of radical reform? It is very easy to be seduced into believing that because some of us are part of an educated, Western liberal elite, consisting of some 0.05 per cent of the world's population, that this male behavioural pattern is a thing of the past. In Japan, until recently, some seventy-five per cent of all marriages were arranged in some form. Matchmakers were still common in the West of Ireland up to twenty-five years ago, old farmers marrying young girls in order not to die without heirs. Ethnic cleansing takes place in Bosnia fifty years after the world proclaimed that the lesson of Hitler had been learned. There is a Sly/Petruchio lurking in us all – brainwashing, processing, hunting, hounding. The old Elizabethan adage that England was 'hell for horses, purgatory for servants, but a paradise for women' was and is simply not true. And what is this Maze torture technique that Petruchio employs in the taming house?

> PETRUCHIO: Thus have I politicly begun my reign,
> And 'tis my hope to end successfully.
> My falcon now is sharp and passing empty,
> And till she stoop she must not be full-gorged,
> For then she never looks upon her lure.
> Another way I have to man my haggard,
> To make her come and know her keeper's call,
> That is, to watch her, as we watch these kites
> That bate and beat and will not be obedient.
> She eat no meat today, nor none shall eat.
> Last night she slept not, nor tonight she shall not.
> As with the meat, some undeservèd fault
> I'll find about the making of the bed,
> And here I'll fling the pillow, there the bolster,
> This way the coverlet, another way the sheets.
> Ay, and amid this hurly I intend
> That all is done in reverend care of her.
> And, in conclusion, she shall watch all night,
> And if she chance to nod I'll rail and brawl,
> And with the clamour keep her still awake.
> This is a way to kill a wife with kindness,
> And thus I'll curb her mad and headstrong humour.
> He that knows better how to tame a shrew,
> Now let him speak – 'tis charity to show.

> (Act IV, Scene i)

The speech itself demonstrates the classic taming technique of bringing a falcon to hand – a falcon, a bird of prey, sharp talons, beak, claws, bringing it to rest on your wrist. No food, no sleep, deprivation. Waking the prisoner at four in the morning, shining the light in the eyes. Just as she is nodding off, drag the bolster away. No food, no sleep, disorientation. The technique has come down through the ages as part of the Political Prisoner Handy Torture Manual, direct from *The Taming of the Shrew*. This speech leaves no doubt as to the seriousness of Petruchio's intentions. It is a revenge play, a revenge dream, not in the classic, Jacobean sense of revenge, but of a man perpetrating revenge on a woman for being in a position of authority over him. Kate finally cracks:

> **KATHERINA: I know it is the moon.**
> **PETRUCHIO: Nay, then you lie. It is the blessèd sun.**
> **KATHERINA: Then, God be blessed, it is the blessèd sun.**
> **But sun it is not, when you say it is not,**
> **And the moon changes even as your mind.**
> **What you will have named, even that it is,**
> **And so it shall be so for Katherine.**

> (Act IV, Scene v)

If black is white, then that is what Kate will swear to. The taming trial is on the last leg.

And so to the wedding feast. As with all the plays, the final scene is riddled with visible and invisible bullets. No happy ending this, but fraught with sexual and social implication.

The guests: Lucentio, now married to 'the Prize', Bianca; Hortensio, Petruchio's best friend, married to a rich widow; Baptista; Gremio, the erstwhile octogenarian suitor; Tranio, now once more Lucentio's servant; Grumio.

It is the postprandial scene of brandy and cigars, the male province rather than the female. The moment when the ladies disappear leaving the gentlemen to the port – the male club. It begins with Petruchio saying, 'Nothing but sit and sit and eat and eat.' Boredom and ennui are already setting in for Petruchio. The chase, the excitement of the kill are over. He's restless; this inactivity is foreign to him.

BAPTISTA: Padua affords this kindness, son Petruchio.
PETRUCHIO: Padua affords nothing but what is kind.
HORTENSIO: For both our sakes, I would that word were true.

(Act V, Scene ii)

What's up with Hortensio? He's only just got married to a rich widow. Is he having a rough time already? It certainly doesn't sound like Padua is being very kind to him.

PETRUCHIO: Now, for my life, Hortensio fears his widow.
WIDOW: Then never trust me if I be afeard.
PETRUCHIO: You are very sensible, and yet you miss my sense:
I mean Hortensio is afeard of you.
WIDOW: He that is giddy thinks the world turns round.
PETRUCHIO: Roundly replied.
KATHERINA: Mistress, how mean you that?
WIDOW: Thus I conceive by him.
PETRUCHIO: Conceives by me! How likes Hortensio that?
HORTESNIO: My widow says this she conceives her tale.
PETRUCHIO: Very well mended. Kiss him for that, good widow.
KATHERINA: 'He that is giddy thinks the world turns round'
I pray you tell me what you meant by that.
WIDOW: Your husband, being troubled with a shrew,
Measures my husband's sorrow by his woe.
And now you know my meaning.
KATHERINA: A very mean meaning.
WIDOW: Right, I mean you.
KATHERINA: And I am mean, indeed, respecting you.
PETRUCHIO: To her, Kate!
HORTENSIO: To her, widow!

What an atmosphere. From the first moment of what should start as a celebration, the knives are out. The needles are digging in, the fur is flying. And something in Petruchio's personality at this moment, leads us to suspect that he is looking for some action, and at precisely this moment, as the two women start to quarrel with each other, so the betting starts, as in the Induction – only for dogs, substitute wives. The husbands are now the hunters. Due to the smallness of casts, usually not more than fifteen or so in Shakespeare's day, this would have been made even clearer by the doubling of roles.

> PETRUCHIO: A hundred marks, my Kate does put her down.
> HORTENSIO: That's my office.
> PETRUCHIO: Spoke like an officer – ha' to thee, lad. [*Drinks*]
> BAPTISTA: How likes Gremio these quick-witted folks?
> GREMIO: Believe me, sir, they butt together well.
> BIANCA: Head and butt! An hasty-witted body
> Would say your head and butt were head and horn.
> VINCENTIO: Ay, mistress bride, hath that awakened you?
> BIANCA: Ay, but not frighted me, therefore I'll sleep again.
> PETRUCHIO: Nay, that you shall not. Since you have begun,
> Have at you for a bitter jest or two.
> BIANCA: Am I your bird? I mean to shift my bush,
> And then pursue me as you draw your bow.
> You are welcome all.

Sweet little Bianca, once the prize, the pride and joy of Baptista, whom everybody lusted after, dressed in her frills, she who plied her music, now has the ring on her finger and is unafraid to speak out, say her piece. Put the men down. Sweet little Bianca suddenly reveals a vicious streak: 'An hasty-witted body / Would say your head and butt were head and horn.' You stupid berk. I mean 'to shift my bush'. Pre-marriage, yes. Post-marriage, no. She sweeps out, shifts her bush, a deliberate, ominous sexual pun. Don't get clever with me, baby, or you won't get any pie tonight. The other women follow in a show of solidarity. The point is made that the women, now that they are married, have obtained social and sexual power. If those are the only rules by which this macho game can be played, so be it.

> PETRUCHIO: Here, Signor Tranio,
> This bird you aimed at, though you hit her not –
> Therefore a health to all that shot and missed.

Note the repetition of the hunting images; Tranio continues the metaphor:

> TRANIO: Oh sir, Lucentio slipped me like his greyhound,
> Which runs himself, and catches for his master.
> PETRUCHIO: A good swift simile, but something currish.
> TRANIO: 'Tis well, sir, that you hunted for yourself.
> 'Tis thought your deer does hold you at a bay.
> BAPTISTA: O, O, Petruchio! Tranio hits you now.
> LUCENTIO: I thank thee for that gird, good Tranio.
> HORTENSIO: Confess, confess, hath he not hit you here?
> PETRUCHIO: 'A has a little galled me, I confess;
> And as the jest did glance away from me,
> 'Tis ten to one it maimed you two outright.

Hunting, betting, gambling images are all intertwined.

> PETRUCHIO: . . . And therefore for assurance
> Let's each one send unto his wife,
> And he whose wife is most obedient,
> To come at first when he doth send for her,
> Shall win the wager which we will propose.
> HORTENSIO: Content. What's the wager?
> LUCENTIO: Twenty crowns.
> PETRUCHIO: Twenty crowns?
> I'll venture so much of my hawk or hound,
> But twenty times so much upon my wife.
> LUCENTIO: A hundred then.
> HORTENSIO: Content.
> PETRUCHIO: A match! 'Tis done.
> HORTENSIO: Who shall begin?
> LUCENTIO: That will I. Biondello,
> Go bid your mistress come to me.
> BIONDELLO: I go.
> BAPTISTA: Son, I'll be your half Bianca comes.
> LUCENTIO: I'll have no halves. I'll bear it all myself.

Even Baptista wants to get in on the act. So, Bianca and the wives of Hortensio and Lucentio are sent for and refuse to come. This is already a reversal of the roles they occupied in the early part of the play when they would never have dreamt of refusing to obey. Kate acquiesces.

> LUCENTIO: Here is a wonder, if you talk of a wonder.
> HORTENSIO: And so it is. I wonder what it bodes.
> BAPTISTA: Now fair befall thee, good Petruchio!
> The wager thou hast won, and I will add
> Unto their losses twenty thousand crowns –
> Another dowry to another daughter,
> For she is changed, as she had never been.
> PETRUCHIO: Nay, I will win my wager better yet,
> And show more sign of her obedience,
> Her new-built virtue and obedience.

The betting continues. Petruchio has gained into the bargain twenty thousand crowns. Money rules. But still he wants more.

> See where she comes, and brings your froward wives
> As prisoners to her womanly persuasion.
> Katherine, that cap of yours becomes you not.
> Off with that bauble, throw it under foot.
> WIDOW: Lord, let me never have a cause to sigh
> Till I be brought to such a silly pass!

This widow is not going to knuckle down for anybody's money.

> BIANCA: Fie, what a foolish duty call you this?
> LUCENTIO: I would your duty were as foolish too!
> The wisdom of your duty, fair Bianca,
> Hath cost me a hundred crowns since supper-time.
> BIANCA: The more fool you for laying on my duty.

How stupid can you get? A gross insult to my intelligence to bet a hundred crowns on blind obedience.

> PETRUCHIO: Katherine, I charge thee, tell these headstrong women
> What duty they do owe their lords and husbands.
> WIDOW: Come, come, you're mocking. We will have no telling.
> PETRUCHIO: Come on, I say, and first begin with her.
> WIDOW: She shall not.

The widow and Bianca do not want to be part of this humiliating process. They have gained some measure of independence by another route. They demonstrate that they now possess a quality, strength and position that they are not prepared to relinquish. Katherina is the one who must now turn turtle and be submissive. Role reversal yet again. Bianca and the Widow are no shrews. They merely show how to bend the marital system to their will, using their newly acquired positions of wealth and power to assert their freedom of will. Blind obedience means to be treated like an animal, degrading and inhuman.

And so to the final speech. In recent years these forty lines or so have probably caused more dispute than any other scene in the complete canon of world drama.

> KATHERINA: Fie, fie, unknit that threatening unkind brow,
> And dart not scornful glances from those eyes
> To wound thy lord, thy king, thy governor.
> It blots thy beauty as frosts do bite the meads,
> Confounds thy fame as whirlwinds shake fair buds,
> And in no sense is meet or amiable.
> A woman moved is like a fountain troubled,
> Muddy, ill-seeming, thick, bereft of beauty,
> And while it is so, none so dry or thirsty
> Will deign to sip or touch one drop of it.
> Thy husband is thy lord, thy life, thy keeper,
> Thy head, thy sovereign; one that cares for thee,
> And for thy maintenance; commits his body

To painful labour both by sea and land,
To watch the night in storms, the day in cold,
Whilst thou liest warm at home, secure and safe;
And craves no other tribute at thy hands
But love, fair looks, and true obedience –
Too little payment for so great a debt.
Such duty as the subject owes the prince,
Even such a woman oweth to her husband.
And when she is froward, peevish, sullen, sour,
And not obedient to his honest will,
What is she but a foul contending rebel
And graceless traitor to her loving lord?
I am ashamed that women are so simple
To offer war where they should kneel for peace,
Or seek for rule, supremacy, and sway,
When they are bound to serve, love, and obey.
Why are our bodies soft, and weak, and smooth,
Unapt to toil and trouble in the world,
But that our soft conditions and our hearts
Should well agree with our external parts?
Come, come, you froward and unable worms,
My mind hath been as big as one of yours,
My heart as great, my reason haply more,
To bandy word for word and frown for frown.
But now I see our lances are but straws,
Our strength as weak, our weakness past compare,
That seeming to be most which we indeed least are.
Then vail your stomachs, for it is no boot,
And place your hands below your husband's foot.
In token of which duty, if he please,
My hand is ready, may it do him ease.

(Act V, Scene ii)

This closing speech of submission is often seen (and delivered) as the expression of a woman now at peace with her husband and herself, a private communication between husband and wife. Countless actors and actresses alike following this tradition have grappled to come to terms with the unpalatable sentiment expressed therein, explaining away the immense distance between the overt sense and the latent subtext as Kate's discovery of her self-expression. But if, when Kate ultimately achieves the power of speech, the result appears to be that of a dog barking to order, what has Petrucio's brainwashing actually achieved? The speech, delivered to the assembled throng, is three times as long as any other in the play – embarrassingly long. The language of subservience is unending. It is embarrassing, not merely for its sentiments in a modern context but deliberately so on the part of Kate. You want excess? You can have it. The moon is the sun if you say it is. You want obedience? Well, get an earful of this. I'll obey so well you won't know what's hit you. It is inexorable. Insistent. If there is a spark of independence left in Kate (and of course there must be) then the speech is ironic. Anything rather than go through all that again. The subtext of the speech is an overt challenge to Petrucio's masculinity.

* * *

Padua, where men come to wive it wilfully, where daughters are deemed 'a Prize' and are put up for auction, where women who step out of line are brutalised into submission, is a competitive grasping cynical city. A city where well-fed men slouch indolently over their port braying 'hear hear' when one of their number extracts a particularly ignominious confession of inferiority from his woman. A city where the sound of the hunting horn echoes symbolically over the walls. A city where a man as unscrupulously deadly as Sly/Petruchio is sure to thrive. But every action has its counter-action. It is to the new-found independence of Bianca and the Widow, finding the humiliation of Kate abhorrent, that we must look to understand the real nature of Sly's wish-fulfilment dream of revenge. The state of blind submission that Katherina finds herself in is how Sly would like his woman (and women) to be. The reality is something different. If there is a journey at all then it is Sly/Petrucio that has made it. As he collects his winnings (making him now even wealthier) and leads his wife back to her kennel at his heel, was that over-the-top speech something of an embarrassment to him? What has he ended up with? Is this what he wanted? But the dream is over and as the Tapster accompanies Sly to his home, we await the sequel, as yet unwritten, as Sly tries to put into action what he has discovered in his dream. Now that would be funny.

Michael Bogdanov
Shakespeare Productions

1970/1 Assistant Director Royal Shakespeare Company (RSC) to John Barton, Terry Hands, Trevor Nunn, David Jones, Robin Phillips, Peter Brook (*A Midsummer Night's Dream* – Associate Director on World Tour).

1971 *Two Gentleman of Verona* (Os Dos Cabelleros di Verona). Teatro Ruth Escobar, Sao Paulo Brazil.

1972 *The Tempest*, Newcastle Playhouse. Designer – Stephanie Howard. Prospero – Bill Wallis.

1974 *Twelfth Night*, The Phoenix Theatre, Leicester. Designer – Mike Bearwish. Olivia – Heather Sears. Orsino – Darryl Forbes-Dawson.

1974 *Romeo and Juliet*, Haymarket Theatre, Leicester. Designer – Adrian Vaux. Romeo – Jonathan Kent. Juliet – Mary Rutherford. Mercutio – Bill Wallis. Paris – Alan Rickman.

1975 *Hamlet*, The Phoenix Theatre, Leicester. Designer – Paul Bannister. Hamlet – Hugh Thomas. Claudius – Bill Wallis.

1975 *'He That Plays the King'* Trilogy; *Richard III, Hamlet, The Tempest*. The Phoenix Theatre, Leicester. Designer – Paul Bannister. Hamlet, Prospero and Richard III – Bill Wallis.

1978   *The Taming of the Shrew*, RSC, Stratford. Designer – Chris Dyer. Petruchio – Jonathan Pryce. Katherina – Paula Dionissotti. Grumio – David Suchet. Tranio – Ian Charleson. Bianca – Zoe Wannamaker.

1979   The 'Action Man' Trilogy, *Hamlet, The Tempest, Richard III* – The Young Vic Theatre, London. Designer – Paul Bannister. Hamlet – Phil Bowen. Richard III and Prospero – Bill Wallis.

1979   *The Taming of the Shrew* – RSC, The Aldwych Theatre, London. Cast as before. (Society of West End Theatres (SWET) Director of the Year Award.)

1980   The 'Action Man' Trilogy, The Old Vic Theatre, London. Hamlet – Tony Milner. Richard III and Prospero – Bill Wallis.

1982   *Macbeth*, a National Theatre Educational Touring Production. Macbeth – Greg Hicks.

1983   *Romeo and Juliet*, The Imperial Theatre, Tokyo, Japan. Designer – Chris Dyer.

1984   *Hamlet*, The Abbey Theatre, Dublin. Designer – Juliet Watkinson. Hamlet – Stephen Brennan.

1985   *Measure for Measure*, The Stratford Memorial Theatre, Ontario, Canada. Designer – Chris Dyer. The Duke – Alan Scarfe.

1986   *Julius Caesar*, Deutsches Schauspielhaus, Hamburg (The National Theatre). Designer – Chris Dyer. Brutus – Michel Degen. Cassius – Dietrich Mattausch. Antony – Uli Tukur.

1986   *The Henrys*, The English Shakespeare Company (ESC). Designers – Chris Dyer and Stephanie Howard. Hal and Henry V – Michael Pennington. Falstaff – John Woodvine.

1986   *Romeo and Juliet*, RSC. Designer – Chris Dyer. Romeo – Sean Bean. Juliet - Niamh Cusack. Mercutio – Michael Kitchen. Tybalt – Hugh Quarshie.

1987   *Romeo and Juliet*, The Barbican Theatre, London. Cast – as before.

1987–1989   *The Wars of the Roses*, ESC World Tour. Designers – Chris Dyer and Stephanie Howard. Richard II, Hal and Henry V – Michael Pennington. Henry VI – Paul Brennan. Richard III – Andrew Jarvis. Falstaff – Barry Stanton. (Laurence Olivier Award for Best Director.)

1989   *Hamlet*, The Deutsches Schauspielhaus, Hamburg. Designer – Bill Dudley. Hamlet – Uli Tukur. Claudius – Christian Redl. Gertrude – Ilse Ritter.

1990   *Romeo and Juliet*, Deutsches Schauspielhaus, Hamburg. Designer – Chris Dyer. Romeo – Marcus Bluhm. Juliet – Catrin Striebeck. Tybalt – Hugh Quarshie. Lady Capulet – Monica Bleibtreu. Capulet – Christain Redl. Nurse – Christa Berndl.

1990   *Coriolanus* and *The Winter's Tale*, ESC World Tour. Designers – Chris Dyer and Claire Lyth. Coriolanus and Leontes – Michael Pennington (TMA Best touring Production).

1991   *The Tempest*, The Deutsches Schauspielhaus, Hamburg. Designer – Chris Dyer. Prospero – Uli Wildgruber.

1992 *Macbeth*, ESC. Designer – Claire Lyth. Macbeth – Michael Pennington. Lady Macbeth – Jenny Quayle.

1992 *Macbeth*, ESC; a landrover tour of Sierra Leone, Ghana, Namibia, Malawi. Designer – Claire Lyth.

1992 *Macbeth* and *The Tempest*, ESC World Tour. Macbeth – Tony Haygarth. Lady Macbeth – Lynne Farleigh. Prospero – John Woodvine.

1994 *Romeo and Juliet*, ESC. Designer – Chris Dyer. Romeo – Jo Dixon. Juliet – Joanna Roth.

1997 *Timon of Athens*. The Chicago Shakespeare Theatre, Chicago. Designer – Ralph Koltai. Timon – Larry Yando.

1997 *Macbeth*, Bayerisches Staatsschauspiel, Munich, Germany. Designer – Claire Lyth. Macbeth – Uli Tukur.

1998 *Anthony and Cleopatra* and *As You Like It*, ESC, Bath Shakespeare Festival. Designers – Geraldine Bunzl and Yannis Thavoris. Anthony – Tim Woodward. Cleopatra – Cathy Tyson. Rosalind – Ivy Omere.

2000 *Troilus and Cressida*, The Bell Shakespeare Company for the Olympics Arts Festival, Sydney Opera House, Australia. Designers – Michael Scott-Mitchell and Ulrike Engelbrecht. Troilus – Toby Truslove, Cressida – Blazey Best. Pandarus – Bille Brown.

2002 *The Merry Wives of Windsor*, Ludlow Festival. Designer – Chris Dyer. Falstaff – Philip Madoc.

2003   *The Winter's Tale*, Chicago Shakespeare Theatre, Chicago. Designers – Derek McClane and Claire Lyth. Leontes – John Reeger. Hermione – Barbara Robertson.

2003   *The Merchant of Venice* and *The Winter's Tale,* The Ludlow Festival Designers – Chris Dyer and Mel Wing. Leontes – Russell Gomer. Hermione – Nickie Rainsford. Shylock – Philip Madoc. Portia – Heledd Baskerville.

TV & Film

1982   *Shakespeare Lives*, Channel 4. Twelve-part series live from the Roundhouse, London.

1987   *Julius Caesar*, ZDF, Germany.

1995   *Shakespeare on the Estate,* BBC Bard on the Box series. (Royal Television Society Award for the Best Documentary.)

1996   *The Tempest in Butetown* – 90 minute feature film for BBC with the residents of Tiger Bay, Cardiff.

1997   *Macbeth,* Granada – Channel 4. Macbeth – Sean Pertwee. Lady Macbeth – Greta Scacchi. Malcolm – Jack Davenport. Banquo – Michael Maloney.

2003   *The Welsh in Shakespeare*, BBC 60-minute drama documentary with Michael Sheen, Philip Madoc, Mark Lewis Jones.

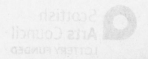

Spring 2004 Titles
Six Contemporary Plays

Dr Korczak's Example - David Greig ISBN: 0-9545206-1-0

King Matt - Stephen Greenhorn ISBN: 0-9545206-2-9

The Waltzer - Rhiannon Tise ISBN: 0-9545206-3-7

Kaahini - Maya Chowdhry ISBN: 0-9545206-4-5

Sunburst Finish - Andrea Gibb and Paddy Cunneen ISBN: 0-9545206-5-3

The Life of Stuff - Simon Donald ISBN: 0-9545206-6-1

PRICE: **£5.99 each**
PAGES: **80 including introduction by author**
PUBLICATION DATE: **May 2004**
DISTRIBUTOR: **Booksource - Tel 0870 240 2182**

Scottish
Arts Council
LOTTERY FUNDED